T'internet Dating?......
Yeah Rite!!

Tara Meredith

authorHOUSE®

AuthorHouse™ UK Ltd.
500 Avebury Boulevard
Central Milton Keynes, MK9 2BE
www.authorhouse.co.uk
Phone: 08001974150

First published by AuthorHouse 3/16/2011

ISBN: 978-1-4567-7453-0 (sc)

Preface

The author of this book (me) is a single (divorced for many years) lady in her mid to late forties. I have a 20 year old son who still lives with me from my charade of a marriage (which didn't last too long unfortunately or fortunately, due to the fact that HE couldn't keep IT in his trousers!). I am a professional lady educated to Masters level, works hard, has lots of friends, has a busy, relatively happy life, BUT...... with one thing missing! Yes you guessed it, that special soul mate that we all search for in our lives at some point!!

This book attempts to capture the memorable and meaningful highlights of my journey and that of my friends and my friends friends, who have been and a few who are still in search of their soul mate!

This collation of **true** male encounters takes you into what I can only describe as the various corners and crevices of the "T'internet" dating scene.!!!! Oh my, have I had my eyes opened!!!!!

Hold on tight to your surfboard and brace yourself for what I would guess are new experiences and insights which will hopefully guide, or at least give all those food for thought, who are on the "T'internet" dating scene, or indeed are thinking of getting involved!

This book may be of interest to those also **NOT** involved or interested in the "T'internet dating scene as they are happily married, living with someone or have a long term relationship but under a separate roof!! **Why?** You may ask! Well, surprisingly or not, I was rather shocked at the number of guys who are on 'normal' and the more dodgy/riske dating websites who admit to being married or have a long term relationship, and still have a need to have a Bit On The Side (BOTS). If I were to put a figure on it, I would best guess that I am talking about 65% overall – no wonder the t'internet dating scene seems to have such a tarnished reputation!! There must be a 'drop-down' option when creating a personal profile as quite a few say that their status is "unhappily married"!!!…… so go your own ways then!! Or am I being too simplistic?? It is also surprising to see the number of guys who feel a need to expose their 'family jewels' on either or both their profile picture or live web-cams! (well I suppose this is a way of not being identified by partners!!)

I really hope you enjoy this book as much as I have enjoyed writing it!!

Enjoy ☺

Acknowledgements

I would like to thank all those who have been ready to share openly their experiences (and yes they WILL remain anonymous!) and hope they also enjoy the read upon completion of this book!

I would also like to thank my close friends for encouraging me to actually write about my experiences and those of others as they said it would be a 'Best Seller'! given the hilarious and thought provoking situations both I and others have found ourselves in!!

I also thank the dating and social networking websites for being there, as without them, this book would not exist!

Keep on surfing!

Introduction

I decided to write this book in a slightly different way, in that I am going to take a 'case study' approach and describe each encounter as accurately as possible as experienced by me or told to me by other ladies out there!

I did actually find my soul mate on t'internet, and that is where I am going to start....... at the end!   The different encounters described thereafter are not necessarily in a chronological order, but themed or in the order in which I found out about them or experienced them, so .... here goes!

Oh, by the way, some of the names are real and some fictional! Either way, only those who were involved in the encounter will know it's them!

My soul mate

Like I said earlier, I did find my soul mate on t'internet just over 6 years ago!

He was on the AOL dating website...... (free membership) and I recall that he contacted me. We chatted for a couple of weeks or so and made arrangements to meet one lunch time for a coffee. He only lived about 2 miles away from where I worked which was rather handy, so I agreed to call round to his pad one Thursday lunch time. He told me that he lived in a 10 bedroom farmhouse and gave me the directions (I did let a friend know where I was going at the time). 'Wow' I thought, he is 6'1" tall, slim, dark hair and from what I could see on his profile, looked pretty dishy! "Kerching!" - is this THE one? I had to give myself a real good talking to (I very often have my own team meetings!) to avoid getting too excited and hopeful and reminded myself to keep my feet firmly on the ground!!

So, this particular lunch time, I made sure I had put a sexy pair of heels on and one of my slightly shorter skirts (just above the knee as opposed to a skirt that covered my ankles!) from the collection of items which made up various ways of wearing my work suit. Off I toddled in my car and must have driven past his house about 4 times before I worked out which farm it was! I drove into this 'square' which consisted of a fish pond (allegedly 10ft deep just out of interest and full of coy carp!), the pond was surrounded by a grassed area which was surrounded by a circular gravelled type drive way all of which was enclosed by what appeared to be unused stables and outbuildings which must have been used to keep cattle and a milking parlour at some stage. As I switched off my engine and glanced to my left (which is where the farm house was) this tall handsome guy emerged wearing designer gear - a cream high neck sweater, a pair of funky denim jeans and a pair of tan, Italian handmade leather shoes (shoes say a lot about a man). "Amazing!" I thought to myself! "I think I've hit the jackpot" As I walked towards him I noticed through his 'power glasses' that he had a glide in one eye so wasn't quite sure where he was looking!! "Oh well" I thought to myself, nobody can be perfect and I'm sure I can get used to the feeling of him always looking elsewhere with one eye if we get on!! (I should have seen this as a sign from whichever angel was looking down on me at that time!)

He gave me a peck on my cheek and invited me into this huge farmhouse where he made me a coffee and we sat chatting, well I say 'we', I went into interview mode and did all the asking! I really wanted to know about this guy!

He had been married twice, had two boys from his first marriage, no kids from his second marriage, and had recently split for a long term relationship with a girl who lived locally. He did explain to me at the time that he was unique and a different character than maybe I had known before!!! Mmmmmm, he wasn't wrong there was he!!!

We were together for about 2.5 years I think, with a few breaks where he did a disappearing trick for a few weeks at a time!! Explanation?...... He told me he had money troubles and when he has to 'sort things out' he has to be on his own as this is the only way he can deal with stuff when it goes wrong! OK, whatever I thought! The first time he re-appeared he apologised and said that he thought he owed me a valentines present (he decided to disappear on Valentines' day which resulted in my being on my jack jones that evening!) OK, I thought, give him a chance! So he went on to say that he would like to take me away for the weekend to Barcelona! I was soooo excited! By this time we had seen each other (before he disappeared) on a number of occasions and every time we went out or stayed in we just got on like a house on fire! So inevitably feelings for this guy just appeared out of the blue, so when he disappeared on Valentines' day, I was absolutely gutted! Which proved to me that I was falling for him already! (they say love is blind!! Oh boy, how right they are, whoever 'they' are!!)

I stayed over at his on the Thursday night ready to leave for Liverpool airport on the Friday (note the date was 1st April!!! April Fool! - more signs) for a 6am flight to Barcelona on 'squeezy jet' - wow, how good was he in bed! Well endowed, a six pack (he was training for his black belt at the time) and knew what to do with it!! Phew!! Amazing is all I can say! The chemistry was definitely there!! Before we left in the morning, I noticed that the light shade on the ceiling light just above the bed was 'wonky', I smiled to myself as I realised that he must have knocked it with his head when in 'doggy' position last night. Ooooer! I thought as I reflected on the passionate and hot few hours we had indulged in as I duly straightened the shade before leaving the house!

We stayed in the 5 star Marina hotel which was stunning! We did nothing but laugh all weekend, it was THE best weekend of my life! The sun was shining, Las Ramblas was busy, and as we strolled towards a tapas bar I realised that I had fallen for this guy BIG time! I was sooooo happy! The next few hours were spent chilling and chatting and laughingin the tapas bar, so a few vinos later we were happy bunnies, nothing else mattered in the world apart from the fact that we were together! "I'm so glad I gave him another chance" I said to myself.

As we had planned to go to the casino on the first night, which meant that it would be a late night, we decided to go back to the hotel for a 'siesta'. As we walked back hand in hand to the hotel he stopped walking, turned towards me and pulled me gently into his arms. He kissed me on the lips and looked deep into my eyes and said "I love you"….. oh my god! I WAS in heaven, I felt as though I could have flown to the moon unaided by any NASA rocket! I told him that I loved him too! We were just soooo happy I could have died!

We would see each other every few days and spent most weekends together, chilling, walking, shopping and most of all out dancing!! At one point somebody in the crowd took a photo of us dancing - a bit of 'dirty dancing' going on - we were amazing together!!! That bloody light shade over his bed did bug me though as it tended to always be on a skew!!! (which I always put straight! - more clues but no real evidence!!!!) He did do a couple more disappearing acts again over the 2.5 years, and yes I gave him another few chances and desperately wanted to believe that he was telling me the truth about the way in which he dealt with his financial problems!! The fourth time we got back together he told me that he had had to move to a smaller property as he couldn't afford the rental on the 10 bedroom farmhouse (yes he did say it was rented but with a view to buying it - he certainly gave the impression that money was not a problem - until now!!)

I arranged to meet him at his new house, which I could only describe as a matchbox compared to his previous digs - it was clear to me that this was a HUGE blow to his ego - it didn't matter to me, I loved him with all my heart and soul, I didn't care what he had or didn't have - together we would make it! (how gullible and naïve was I?) So, he had moved house and was trying to attract more business (self-employed) to increase his earnings - OK I thought, let's just get on with life together as it is. That Christmas was difficult due to lack of funds for him, and guess what, he disappeared again!!! How many chances does this guy want? I was gutted yet again, another Christmas on my own!! On Boxing Day I received a txt from him apologising and asking to see me - he was really sorry, and pleaded for me to meet with him - he wanted to spend the day with me walking and talking - guess what - I agreed to meet with him!! He certainly had a tight hold of my heart strings!!! We met and walked around the shops on New Years' eve in the rain. It was about 4pm on that day when all of the Christmas lights came on as darkness began to fall - he stopped me next to the huge Christmas tree which was stood under what I can only describe as a cascade of lights which looked like stars against the night sky...... he looked deep into my eyes and said "Next year babes, I'm going to ask you to marry me" he smiled and my heart melted....... Again!!

In the summer of that last year together he took me out for afternoon tea at a very posh hotel for my birthday which was very unexpected and very romantic. We had the usual posh sandwiches with the crusts removed and cut into tiny triangles and cakes with our cups of tea. After about half an hour a waitress came to us with 2 glasses of champagne accompanied by a small box - you know, the type that rings are purchased in!!! NO!!! this can't be happening!! Am I dreaming? Somebody pinch me!!! He looked over at me and he asked "Do you still want to marry me?" I couldn't speak, I just cried with tears of happiness. After a few minutes I managed to get one word out "Yes" I said with the biggest smile in the world!! I was sooooo happy my heart felt like it was going to burst! Everyone was really pleased for us and we started to discuss plans for the future which included him moving into my pad to enable us to save up to relocate and move to Spain which is where we could start a new life running our own business - we spent one Saturday afternoon in the Slug and Lettuce on the squashy sofas designing our restaurant and new home - I still have this to this day!! It was a dream...... a foolish dream on my part!!

For a few months before "D-Day" I had been rather suspicious of a number of things - a clothes ticket (with picture) off some raunchy lingerie which I had found in his en-suite (he said he had found the label in the street and thought it was unusual underwear so he had picked it up and put it in his pocket); a scratch on his back (which he explained was from a garage door he went under); a stretchy bling bracelet in the dash of his car (one son had borrowed his car so must be his girlfriends); a tube of lipstick left in his main bathroom (the other son had had his girlfriend stay the night when he was at mine)...... he always had an answer and I had lack of any real evidence even though my female intuition was telling me to be brave and dig deeper!!! Oh and he would NEVER leave his mobile phone about!!!

The last week we were together I had a conversation with my Grandad, (through the spirit waves!) bless him, he had passed away when I was about 11 years old, however to this day I still chatted to him as I know he is my protector and know he is always with me - so I said to him, "Right Grandad, if there is any evidence of my other half being unfaithful and lying then I want to know about it!!"

On the Friday morning of that week he had left home (his pad) early to go training somewhere in south Wales so he had left me in bed asleep as I didn't have to get up for work for another hour. When I woke up I noticed that the draw on his bedside cabinet was slightly open and revealed his old mobile phone!! I felt sick, was this phone going to be the evidence I had asked to see if it existed? My heart was pounding so hard in my chest that I could hardly breath!....... Had my Grandad heard me and had provided me with this opportunity to find out either way? I had no choice but to look at the phone. I took it out of the draw and attempted to turn it on..... It was dead, no battery power.... I had started so had to finish as Magnus Magnasson used to say on Mastermind, I took the phone downstairs to see if his new phone charger would fit his old phone..... Guess what??

It did!! I felt sicker than I did before…. I plugged it in and whilst waiting a few minutes for it to charge a little, I had a flick through his diary he had left on the dining room table that morning only to find details of a flight to Prague which coincided with one of the occasions he did his disappearing trick!! (I found out later that he had flown to Prague with his ex-girlfriend and saw pics of them hand in hand over the dinner table whilst I was at home gutted!) I had always said to myself that if I ever get to this point of mistrust and suspicion then the relationship could not work!! I turned the phone on and went to his text messages folder….. Not again!! The bottom of my world had collapsed yet again…. There were about 7 different contact details saved as "D" or "J" or "T" or whatever letter, the text messages made it very clear that he had been seeing not just one woman but several! One text read……"Last night was fantastic, however I feel that I am just being used for sex". A text from "T" was a full frontal picture of her private bits with a message "Polite notice - F**k here now" - I felt ill, the hurt I felt inside was indescribable - I could hardly breath!! My eyes involuntarily filled with tears, I couldn't see, I sat and cried and sobbed for ages. Eventually I pulled myself together, went to work, couldn't concentrate, sent him a few texts asking how "T" was as this was the latest contact according to the phone - he rang me and guess what, denied my allegation of him seeing other women!! We met later on that same day, which was the most awful day ever. Eventually he had no option, given the evidence to admit to his lies and the fact that he had been cheating on me since day one! – no wonder that light shade had nearly always been on a skew!!! He had been busy s****ing anything that stood still long enough!! The relationship had to end!!

What hurt the most after seeing him walk away, was that we were so close, he was my soul mate (and always will be) and still wish to this day that he had never lied and cheated as he did! I wish I could put my world into reverse so he would still be by my side, but that's not going to happen!! I will never forget the time when he said to me that he couldn't describe the way in which he felt about me, it was too deep to describe, deeper than his soul! (This was a few months after I had caught him out and after we had been apart for a few months and were still sort of in contact) Perhaps we should have stayed together as I will never know now what the future could have been like - would he have ever changed his ways? Well, you know what they say "A leopard never changes its spots". But then again, could I have lived with that awful feeling every time he answered his phone or went out of the door of asking myself the question "what is he really doing? And where is he really going?" I was told bymy spiritual medium that if I did get back with him, I may as well sit in a dark corner and shoot myself as this would be less painful! Well, as you can see, I chose not to sit in a dark corner and shoot myself, but to live life as best I could without him – c'est la vie, onwards and upwards, things can only get better……. Or can they??!!

Whilst writing this book I did discover that he was living in the same village as me, obviously with another woman, as financially he could not sustain himself!! (no change there then!) I wonder if his current victim…. Ooops, 'partner' knows that he does still send me the odd email asking me when we are going to have a night out 'dirty dancing' again? (I bet on my life she doesn't! and I bet on my life she will NEVER get her hands on his mobile phone!!) He is like a cat with 9 lives crossed with a slippery snake able slip in and out of difficult situations when cornered and still land on his feet!!! (can't go on forever though can it? – watch this space - the truth will out!!!) OK, enough of him, let's move onto some REAL T'internet experiences…. All from a female perspective of course!!

The real estate French Canadian

After some time away from t'internet dating/chatting etc I purchased a new lap top to replace the previous one which had suddenly died. The new laptop obviously came with t'internet access as I would need this for my studies. I joined Friends Reunited to do some tracking of family hierarchy and to see if I could track down any old school mates (Girls Grammar so no guys involved! And no, wasn't thinking of changing my sexual orientation either!!) I kept receiving emails about meeting Mr Right from the website and eventually joined and paid whatever it was for a 3 month membership as this was the better deal. One Sunday afternoon I was sat surfing the web for journals and articles to do with my studies when I received a chat request from this guy called Simon. This was a rather nice surprise and distraction at that point!! Wow, I looked at his profile, he had dark hair, very attractive, 1 son living with grandparents in Canada, ex partner allegedly had done time and now issued with a court order of some sort not to make contact with him.

His emails were very deep and meaningful, he was very attentive and made contact with me daily talking about when he would be able to fly down to Manchester to meet me. Simon lived in Aberdeen so not easy to meet with him as it was a 6 hour drive either way!!

He said he was a real estate developer and that once he had finalised this latest project which was real estate development in China, he would have all the time and money in the world to spend with me. He said he drove a Black Range Rover Sport and had just purchased a mini for his son when he returns from Canada. He asked me about my circumstances, what I did for work, what car I drove etc etc….. One afternoon whilst I was at work Simon rang me on my mobile, his voice was very distinguished, deep, sensuous with a very sexy French Canadian accent!! Wow!! Oh my, I can't wait to meet with him and start a new life with someone special!! He asked me if I had received the flowers he had sent to me at work ….. "No" I said and asked where he had sent them to…. He repeated the address which was accurate, so after the phone call I rang down to main reception to see if they had been sent to the wrong place…. No, nobody had seen any flowers!! Oh well, I'm sure they would turn up at some point!! WRONG!!! They never did, anyway I thought to myself, it's only a bunch of flowers!!

He used to call me every few days to keep me updated and tell me how much he missed me, gosh, I could really fall for this guy and I've not even met him! How can this be? He had also told me that he had fallen for me BIG time and also couldn't wait to hold me in his arms! All the right things were said without being smutty or cheesy!

Every now and again I used to call him, however, the way in which I was connected to him was very strange, I used to get an American voice which said that I was being redirected - Simon explained that he used a satellite phone etc setup for his business and he was in the process of sorting some issues out with his phone provider!! He used to send me some amazing emails and I looked forward to receiving them most days.

Simon explained to me that before he could fly down to Manchester he had to fly to Beijing to meet with some clients to finalise this deal which was worth millions of pounds and once sorted the world was our lobster! Oh my, was this really happening to me? I was soooo excited! He was gorgeous, I really couldn't wait to see him. He told me that it wouldn't take long and he should be able to join me in a few weeks…. OK I thought, a few weeks isn't long to wait really to meet the man of my dreams as we had a long happy future together… hopefully!

On the day he was due to fly to Beijing he sent over his flight details which included his home address in Aberdeen. Great I thought I could send him a birthday card whilst he was away! A nice surprise when he got back!! I checked out the flight details on t'internet, yep, flight existed and was on time, fine, everything is looking good!

One afternoon at work, I was chatting to a work colleague telling him about this guy, his strange phone arrangements and that he was flying over to Beijing to sort out a business deal. My work colleague explained to me that you can actually track down the location of the computer using emails sent to me…….. "No way" I said!! Yes, this is correct and my work colleague duly showed me how to do this. Each computer has an IP address which can be copied from an email header. Later on that day I opened up an email Simon had sent to me when he was in Aberdeen (allegedly) I accessed the email header, copied everything in it and pasted it into a blank box on a website which enabled you to track down the location of the IP address (free of charge)……. I waited for a few seconds, scrolled down to find out where this had been sent from…… ACCRA!!!! Ghana!!! "WHAT?!!" This guy was supposed to be in Aberdeen!!! My heart sank, what was going on? I duly checked out another email he had sent from China, and guess what!!! The IP address was STILL saying ACCRA, Ghana!!! I was in a state of disbelief!!! I decided not to say anything to Simon next time we spoke, I thought that I would see where this was going……. Deep down I knew immediately that this was a con!! DAMN! I was gutted!!

A few weeks passed when I received a call from Simon telling me that he had to fly to Ghana to sort out some issues with the wood supplier for the construction in China. (What a coincidence!!!…… Ghana!) I empathised with him and told him not to worry, I'm sure everything will turn out OK eventually! I told him that I was still looking forward to seeing him very soon!! He told me that he would be staying with a business associate Mr. Duclo and his family and would call me when he could, he told me again that he missed me very much and couldn't wait to spend the rest of his life with me. Ahhhh, how nice is that!!?? (said sarcastically!) - I was intrigued now as to what his next move was going to be.

Time went on and one day he called me to tell me he was very upset and down, there was a problem with the wood supplier…. He explained that due to the fact that the wood was in short supply the price had increased…… and due to the fact that he only dealt in cash (due to his ex-partners misdemeanours) he had a cash flow problem!!!! He went on to ask me if I could send him £4.5K via a money-gram to a Mr. Duclo and duly gave me his details…… Yeah Rite!!! So you think I'm stupid enough to do that!!??……send £4.5K over to a complete stranger, NO CHANCE!!! Well this guy hounded me for weeks and even asked me to open up a HSBC account which he could use to transfer money into from his mothers account!!! Mmmmm, is this called money laundering!?!? Needless to say, I ceased all contact with this guy, who for all I know, was some skinny, black Ghanian guy working in some back street sweat shop, the whole purpose being to con money out of vulnerable single ladies in the UK!!!! Watch out ladies..... Be very aware and careful of these guys!! They are VERY convincing!!! Do NOT send any money anywhere!!!

SCAMS – BEWARE!!!

Here are a few examples of emails received from guys who I believe to be Scam profiles:

Example 1
Hello Angel (no picture on profile!)

Hello there my eight wonder,lol.Where do i start from? Really it is disturbing to come on this dating site to see how much people appreciate love, but yet We have to go the extra mile to get this great status.

Forgive my manners, i am James W******s, an engineer of international repute. I deal basically with oil platforms ranging from Africa to middle east and far east asia. But really i am hanging the hat this year, i think after getting all the wealth in pursuit, i have come to realise that we are nothing without a partner, someone who would stand by me no matter the situation. A woman who i can say, she alone has the right to be womanly irritating to me,lol. A witch who would protect me like a lioness would do her cub,lol. and i can promise to protect her beyond all vices. A woman who tells me, honey, you can do it,. no matter what i want to do. I really worked hard the past 12 yrs to get this height.

I have seen faces of women on this site, many of whom have been taken for granted , many of whom are not being reciprocated, but i have come with a good news and a bad news,. the good news is i came here to pick my woman to make happy , my eight wonder, my best friend, my copilot, but the bad news is that i have only one woman to do this for.lol.

I saw something in your face, something that made my heart pause to read you, something that tickles in the heart, could there be love at first sight? maybe we could find that out,lol. You can pls write to me at my personal mail as i may be taking my profile off to avoid identity theft soon. My personal mail is : j********@hotmail.com , i can access that anywhere cos I will not be hear for too long. I'm talking about fate here when feelings are so powerful it's as if some force beyond your control is guiding you to someone who can make you happy beyond your wildest dreams.

your new friend.

James"

What a load of garbage!!…. A witch who would protect him like a lioness protects her cubs!!?? What sort of stories did his parents read to him when he was a child? Lol!

Example 2

"Hi how are you….

i really did enjoy glancing through your profile..You are very pleasing and attracting,i guess no one is going to skip your profile without leaving a message.I am single and in search of a person who understands friendship as truth and faith rather seeing it as a way of fun, but a matured person with good sense of humor,reading about you I felt sincerity in you.your profile gives good recommendation and am well pleased.I will be very happy if we generate easy communication and also know much about each other.I will be looking forward to your respond as I wish you all the best for your day."

This profile did not have any picture on it, he was age 55, single, looking for a serious relationship however lived in California, USA!! Long way to travel each day/week etc!!...... Having looked at more detail contained within his profile, he describes himself as being very attractive, light brown hair, grey eyes, professional qualification, an engineer, 6'6" tall AND weighs 9st 3lbs!!!....... OMG he must be a thin as a matchstick….. or maybe he just got his conversion tables wrong when writing his profile!!! The devil is in the detail!! Keep your eyes peeled ladies for this type of information!!

Example 3

"Hey,

How are you doing? well my name is Chris A****s. Am new here so i went through your profile and i found it lovely and interesting so i wish you go through mine. Am looking for a serious relationship which i believe very soon we'll get along. pls do mail me back when ever you are chance. looking forward hearing from you.

Chris"

This guy also lived in the USA, Illinois, he is aged 44, divorced and looking for a serious relationship. He did have a picture on his profile which looked as though he was overweight, which strangely enough conflicted with his description of being 6'0" tall, athletic build and good looking!!! Well I suppose individual perceptions are very different in some cases!! I would have described him as a couch potato type build and looked like a bit of a baked bean!!! An oval shaped face which had spent too long in the tanning salon!!!

In conclusion areas of commonalities include:

* Most of the time they are Widowed

* They are in the Armed Forces, Consultancy/Sales or Construction/Real Estate

* Normally have Children who live with their grandparents or ex-partner

* Poor English/Grammar/Spelling with a professional qualification

* Live in another country or a million miles away in the UK ie a logistical problem to overcome should you chose to arrange to meet them - this gives them the opportunity to get to know you over the t'internet and whoo you to the point where you send them money!!!

* They fall in love with you online before they have ever met you!

* Ask for money when they think they have captured your heart!

The DJ in denial

Well, it was Friday again and no particular plans made for the weekend, when I received a text message some time in the morning from one of the guys I had been chatting with via email and text for a couple of weeks and he seemed quite nice! He suggested that I come over to his place in the evening and we could have a bottle of wine, chill out in front of the TV and just cuddle up and chat and what have you! Well I thought, I don't really know this guy very well so replied to say that maybe we could do this at some point in the future once we have got to know each other better and we have met in a neutral public place.

I then received a lovely text message saying that he isn't a nutter, gave me his address and postcode, reminded me that we are both adults and it would be good to spend a Friday night not alone! And if I wanted to have a bath and freshen up when I got there then I was more than welcome!

Well ladies what would you have done? I decided to risk it and go round after work for some male company! Needless to say, I dashed into town at lunch time to purchase some make-up, moisturiser, toothpaste and toothbrush, shampoo and conditioner, oh and a travel hair dryer and some perfume! Gosh, this was an expensive date! Hope it's worth while and he is a really nice guy, and who knows HE could be the one!

So all afternoon I'm mmmm-ing and arrrgh-ing as to whether I should actually go round to this guys house, I will call him DJ Shady who in fact was an Ex-DJ who had been 'on the scene' many years ago!

Anyway, the end of the working day arrived and I made my decision to go round to this place having checked out the directions on the RAC route planner already at lunch time – he wasn't too far away.

I piled into my car, shopping and all, and headed off in the direction of his abode. Half an hour later I enter into the road on which he lived, and having quickly scanned the scenery I suddenly started to wonder whether I should do a quick hand-brake turn and scarper! Too late!! He had spotted me!! My mobile phone rang, and as I rightly presumed he **had** spotted me, (good job I answered the phone then!) he was ringing me to direct me to a parking spot opposite his upstairs flat (as I instantly discovered!). So as I drove up the curb of the pavement to position my car behind his Renault Megane to then attempt to make a glamorous exit from my car without getting my heels stuck in the muddy grass which seemed to be the central green the kids played football on.

OK, deep breath then and off I toddled across the road to the corner of this square where DJ Shady was stood waiting for me in the doorway. I walked up the pathway and said hello with a peck on the cheek. He looked rather like Billy Mitchell off Eastenders, slight, suntanned, a bit too wrinkled for his age, short brown hair which was going a bit thin on top. He said 'hello' and directed me up THESE stairs! Oh no! Now, don't forget that I was actually now stood in his 'hall-way' about 2ft square, a door to the left for the downstairs flat and stairs to the right for the upstairs flat

– as I walked up the stairs to the upstairs flat I noticed that the white paint at the edge of the concrete stairs definitely needed another coat of white paint for safety purposes! Oh well, he seems a genuine guy, keep walking and at least have a glass of wine with him!

As I entered the lounge, even though distracted by the extremely loud dance music which was blasting out of one of the music channels, I noticed that it was rather cluttered with all sorts! I felt quite sorry for him as his little gas fire in the centre of the chimney breast struggled to dimly glow from the awful 'covered in nicotine' flowery old fashioned wallpaper which must have been put up when the flats were built in the 60's!

"Never mind, it's a bit of company" I said to myself, stay and have a quick small glass of vino and then run! As we sat 'chatting' about music and other stuff for about an hour I realised that I was asking him after each sentence, to repeat himself as I just could not understand his broad 'scouse' accent (which was extremely fast!) above both the TV which was still at the same volume level (about 60) as when I first arrived AND his old DJ decks which were even louder!! Oh my, this was worse than being in a nightclub in terms of trying to hold a conversation – I wonder what the neighbours were thinking! Well, maybe that's it! They don't think because they are brain dead from living next door to DJ Shady!!

As he went on to show me his collection of posters with his name on and the places he had done his stuff, I eventually got a 'dodgy' glass of wine! It was OK because I saw him open a new bottle of wine and pour it out! It wasn't quite at the standard of Lambrini, (mega cheap hangover gear) but just one stage better than that!!! Disgusting! So I forced myself to have a few sips so as not to seem rude before I explained to him that I didn't feel too good and would have to go!

So 2 hours later, I finally 'left the building' (just like Elvis) hoping that I would never see another green plastic John Smith's ashtray (which he said he had only just emptied as it had been full to the brim) on another makeshift coffee table which was 'engineered' from an old wallpaper paste table with bits missing! Ie bottom half of the legs and half of the fold-up table!

DJ Shady did text me about a week afterwards which read "Hi", I didn't have the inclination or energy to reply to that one so the DJ in denial went into Room 101!

The Jumper

During my early days of surfing the net and in particular social networking sites which included Plenty of Fish (POF) and Friends Reunited (FR) I decided that I would take a different approach and I would consider approaches from different men ie those types I wouldn't have looked at twice which in theory meant avoiding the 'bad boys' as sung by Alexandra Burke and focusing on the 'nice guys'.

When joining a new site it seems that the trend is to get lots of interest which sort of tails off after a while and you get a few persistent guys who would just chat forever online, which is fine, but then after about 6 months of not arranging to meet seems fairly pointless!! So during the initial period of joining a particular website I began chatting to someone called John (John's seem to come in all shapes and sizes and ages!) again, he seemed to be nice chap and we were texting, emailing and actually having telephone conversations for some time and we got on rather well!

On his profile picture (which was rather distant) he looked OK but couldn't quite tell, however I still made a conscious decision to go with it and meet someone rather different than I would normally go for! He looked like he was medium build with dark hair, slightly greying around the edges, an average type of guy really a few inches taller than me.

After about 6 weeks of chatting we made arrangements to meet in a public place, a pub of course which was half-way between where we both lived – all fine so far. We said that we would meet on the car park and therefore we asked each other what type of car we drove, colour etc to make it easier to find each other! John said that he drove a company car which was a Volvo Estate, which immediately conjured up a picture of a boring late middle aged family man, you know, the type who used to live next door to you when you were a child and called him "Uncle" something or other, the one with a purple bulbous nose(from drinking too much sherry), with grey hair and wearing tan coloured nylon socks from British Home Stores. The matching tan coloured sandals used to amuse me as I sometimes sat with him in the back garden peeling pickling onions over a bucket of water! Oh! and usually smelt of those moth-ball things, which I have never seen in my life - do they exist?

Anyway, I drove onto the car park at about 7.30pm looking for this dark blue Volvo estate, and hey presto there it was just to the right of me. John spotted my car and started to walk towards me………. My smile must have looked like a "Wallace" smile, (out of Wallace and Grommit) as I began to talk to myself through my exposed teeth as I continued to smile "oh dear! Here we go again!" I said to myself out loud. He WAS just like my next door neighbour as I have described! "what do I do?" I ask myself! Well, go and have a drink with him, you've been chatting with him for a while now and he's made the effort to actually turn up!

I remove myself from my car as he approaches and he gives me a hug and peck on the cheek and asks me whether or not I still want to go for a drink? Well, I didn't have the heart to say no, so went into the pub for a diet coke!

He went to the bar and I sat down in an old-fashioned high back cosey chair and eventually he perched on a smaller similar chair to the right of me with a round table in front of us. I asked him how long ago was it since his last relationship ended and what happened? (he had probably told me this before but I just had to say something to pass the time away!) John told me that he had been on his own now for about 8 months and the reason why his last relationship ended was because she (don't know her name) kept telling him that she didn't like his jumpers, she didn't like his shirts, she didn't like his trousers, she didn't like this shoes and didn't like his underpants! Well, at this stage I nearly choked on my diet coke! The thought of him in a pair of boxer shorts or Y-fronts was just a big NO NO! I felt rather ill! From that point on all I could do was look straight into his eyes, I didn't dare look at what he was wearing! Oh, my line of sight did have to look a little lower down when he pointed to a yellow splodge on his jumper as he explained that he had had a curry for his tea and had spilt some down his jumper! Oh no! he could have changed it before coming out, but then again, maybe it's the only jumper he owned! It was one of those Pringle golfing jumpers which every golfer over the age of 80 seems to wear!

How I kept my face straight I will NEVER know! We continued to chat for a while and after about 30 minutes he moved his chair a little nearer to me and asked if he could hold my hand! I didn't want to create any feeling of unease for him so just said I didn't mind - well, you shake hands with strangers don't you!

Well, when his hand touched mine, it felt like a bunch of economy out of date chipolatas that had been out of the fridge for half a day! All clammy, sweaty, a little puffed up and lifeless and looked as though they belonged to someone who had just recently died! (still a bit warm and a bit pink! Not that I have touched a dead person's hand!) Another wave of nausea came over me so I immediately shuffled about and moved my hand, at which point John said he was going to go to the Gents! Thank god for that! Perhaps he was going to do a runner and not come back! WRONG! He re-appeared a few minutes later, (I hope he had washed his chipolata hands after handling the goods) however in the meantime it had given me chance to have a good look at his attire! Well, ex-girlfriend, I totally agree with your comments! (apart from the boxer shorts of course!) The polo shirt which was underneath his jumper was frayed around the neck, his jeans looked like a pair of 'BOGOF's' (Buy One Get One Free from the market!) and his shoes! He was wearing a pair of Cornish pasty shoes! The ones that are tan coloured and fold over on one side just like a traditional Cornish pasty! Oh how embarrassing! They say you can always tell a man by the kind of shoes he wears! The only Cornish pasty I like is one on a plate with brown sauce and not the kind laced to the ends of guys legs!

Anyway, he sat back down and we carried on chatting when I suddenly noticed above his eyebrow that he had a fresh cut, so I asked him what he had done. He explained that the evening before he had been reaching for his mobile phone on a table near to him when he slipped on his laminate floor and banged his head on the corner of the table! Oh dear, I said, you were lucky you didn't do any real damage to your eye! At that point I just had this vision of him on his laminate floor, in his boxer shorts, with sparks flying from his tan nylon socks as he did an "Ali-shuffle" on is laminate flooring before going "Dink" on the table! Well I cried with laughter all the way home, rang my friend to explain to her how the date had gone on, which took some time as I was literally speechless! I couldn't get my words out as I was laughing soooo much!

He did ask me before we left the car park whether or not he was going to get a 'Dear John' text afterwards! At this point I owned up and said "Yes, I'm afraid so!" He looked disappointed and text me about an hour later to say he was "gutted". Oh well, I did try a different guy, but it just isn't for me!!

Onwards and upwards – yet again!

NEXT!!! (As they say in Pheonix Nights as the acts audition for the following week!)

On y'er bike!

Stuart and I had been chatting on the website called Smooch which is a free dating site and seemed to have more 'normal' guys on there than the other dodgier sites I had come across!! He lived just outside of Middleton the north east side of Manchester heading towards Leeds, which was about an hour away from where I lived. Stuart worked as a lecturer in Manchester so had a brain, could have a really good conversation and seemed to be an upbeat type of guy!! Just what I was looking for. He was solvent, lived on his own, didn't have any children, never married as he had spent most of his life focusing on his career. Fine, I thought, at least he doesn't have any baggage to bring with him. He was of slim build, mid-forties, didn't smoke, brown hair, brown eyes and a rather tanned complexion from what I could see on his profile picture. All looking good I thought!!

After a few weeks of chatting Stuart suggested meeting up for a bite to eat somewhere that would be convenient for us both… fine, I was thinking maybe Manchester would be best as there were lots of choices of where to eat and lots of people about. He emailed me and suggested we meet at Middleton Services on the M62 on the East Bound side!! Oh my, Burger King and Fries….. Mmmm, not what I had envisaged, but hey, I do quite live a Burger King now and again!! I agreed to meet with him at 6.30 pm which would give me time to leave work and refresh my make-up after a long day at the office. I arrived slightly earlier than planned so decided to go and have a coffee whilst I waited for Stuart to arrive. As I looked out of the window onto the car park I considered myself lucky and glad I had arrived early as the heavens had just opened and it was absolutely lashing it down!! (as it does in the NW!!) At about 6.40 I was still sat looking out of the window and checking my mobile now and again to see if Stuart had left any messages ie he would be a bit late, or if he had changed his mind!! As I reached into my bag for my phone again, I noticed that the restaurant had suddenly gone a little darker... and as I looked to my right I was 'greeted' by this skinny looking guy carrying a racing bike on one shoulder, who looked like a drowned rat. The first thing he said to me is...... "Is there anywhere to put my bike?" I didn't get any "hello's" or "hi, how are you?" just, "Is there anywhere to put my bike?"...... well how the hell did I know, I thought, my name isn't Jeeves!! "Sorry" I said, "I have no idea, spaces are usually at the main entrance" He said that he knew this, but with this being an expensive bike didn't want to leave it in the normal place. He looked around the restaurant for a few seconds until he sussed out where he could leave his bike, which was against a rail with divided the walk way and the diners. I noticed that as he walked away from me his waterproof cape must have been a few years old as it looked warn and had a rip in the back of it. Both of his beige trouser legs were tightly wrapped around his skinny ankles with matching bicycle clips (which he kept on all night) - oh my! Here we go again!!! yet ANOTHER disappointment!!

He quickly parked his bike and chained it to the rail with his padlock, removed his helmet and cape and made his way back over to me..... "Hi" I said "How are you?" "A wee bit wet and cold he said but I will be fine after we have eaten. What do you fancy?" he asked. I said that I would love a Double Bacon Cheeseburger meal with coke. He went over to the serving counter and ordered both of our meals which didn't take long, so he was back with me after about 5 minutes. We sat chatting about the day and what had been happening at work. He was a dry sort of character and very much into his academic subject which was fine art. After about an hour of conversation it was clear to me that the chemistry was not there and it would have been more entertaining to date a cardboard cut out!!

By now the weather had taken a turn for the worse and to add to the torrential rain the wind speed was also on the increase. I asked Stuart if he would like a lift home as the weather was not good for cycling - he smiled and said yes that would be great if I didn't mind!! "Sure, no problem" I replied. Before we made a move to leave, Stuart pushed the Burger King receipt over to me and said that my meal came to £5.50, in other words I was paying for my own!! Blimey, I thought, last of the big spenders!! NOT! I took out my purse and gave him the exact money before I stood up to go. I had already offered him a lift home and this is what I did. He unchained his bike from the rail and carried it over to my car to put it into the boot. Off we went, still east bound on the M62 to the next junction which was about 15 minutes away. He didn't live too far away from the motorway exit which was good as I could easily find my way back to the Junction without getting lost!! We said our "nice to meet you bit and will speak soon" which took about 30 seconds and then gave me a kiss on my cheek. As the weather was still bad he jumped out of the car speedily and ran to his front door for cover.

I reversed my car back onto the road and waved bye to him as he stood under the porch - he waved back! At this point, I felt really sorry for him, he looked very sad and lonely. He sort of had a look of Paddington bear when he was stood alone on the station platform armed with his marmalade sandwich!! Lol!! I turned my wipers on to fast and drove off into the dark dismal night and headed for home. Oh well, another one bites the dust I thought!! Turned my music up, dusted myself down (mentally) ready to start all over again!! Or do I, I'm getting fed up now of these non-descript meetings......!!

After about 20 minutes of driving, I noticed that I had 4 missed calls off Stuart - oh, I wonder what he wants already....... I rang him back to see what the problem was....... Ooops! How could I have missed that? He had only left his bike in my car boot and wanted me to turn around and drop it off!! "Oh for gods sake" I said out loud to myself (after I had ended the call) I'm going to have to carry on until the next junction, turn around go all the way back up the M62 again! I was NOT amused! Needless to say, I duly turned around, dropped his bike off and eventually got home at 10pm - In summary, the cost benefit analysis of this little rendezvous was not worth investing in!! ie the cost of the petrol, Burger King and my time was certainly NOT worth the effort!! So Stuart was never seen again - he never contacted me and I never contacted him..... I was tempted to text him to say... "On yer bike" but I resisted! I was a good girl on this occasion!!

A right Charlie

Well, I did see him! A larger than life Scottish hunk originally from Glasgow, covered in tattoos, worked for the railway and had the most gorgeous eyes EVER! And sexiest tight ass too! I couldn't understand a word he said, but who cares! He was absolutely gorgeous! In my eyes anyway! I would describe him as a rough diamond, but would take a hell of a lot of polishing to transform him into long term boyfriend material! Maybe I just don't think longer term and just have some fun with him now and again, no harm done, nobody else hurt!

We arranged to meet on a night out in Manchester one summer evening - he was out with the lads from work and I was out with the girls. As soon as our eyes met (and his eyes met my boobs! I was wearing a white cotton halter neck top which did show off my cleavage rather well I have to say!) we hit it off big time! The chemistry was certainly there. The night ended up with a gang of 8 of us going for a huge pub crawl around the city - it was a great night and I really liked this guy - Charlie.

On our first night out I was asking him about his past and what he had been doing with his life so far, as you do to get to know about someone. He said that he had been up and down the country working for the railway, however when he was younger, in his 20's I think, he told me that he had done time for about 6 months which was for drug dealing! After getting over the initial shock and thinking about prison as a way of rehabilitating and realising the error of your ways, I asked the intellectual question "With hindsight, what would he have done differently when he was that age?" I braced myself for a lengthy response about reflection and lessons learned! WRONG! I had a 3 word response "Not get caught!"

We met fairly often, usually twice a week for a few months, which often involved DRINK! And when it didn't involve drink it would be a quick rendezvous at lunch time. If I was at home and not in work he would pop round to see me at lunch time when he was on the "MacDonald's Run", no that isn't his surname, he used to go out and get the burgers and chips for the guys he was working with! Needless to say, whenever it was his turn to get the burgers, there was ALWAYS a long queue!! (that's what he told the guys anyway!)

Well one Saturday night we decided to go on a 'bender' around the local village...... have you ever tried to keep pace with a Glaswegian 6'O" hunk? Well I did! Oh and didn't I suffer the next day ☹ It must have been that Viagra and fresh air mixed with the alcohol that gave me amnesia! The definition of amnesia in the English dictionary is "memory loss: loss of memory as a result of shock, injury, psychological disturbance, or medical disorder" Hilarious, I would definitely say that my memory loss was as a result of shock and psychological disturbance after a night out with Glaswegian Charlie!! I couldn't remember a bloody thing after about midnight! I must have had a good night thereafter as I woke up completely naked with my toes on the pillow next to his tattooed shoulders - good job I had painted my toe nails the night before!

A week or so later one of my close friends asked me again to describe Charlie which I did "6'0" tall, muscular, light brown hair, very short, gorgeous blue eyes, broad Scottish accent, covered in tattoos (not on his face or neck but everywhere else!). She went on to say that on this particular day she had been at the travel agents near to stoke and whilst they (her and her husband) were booking their holiday, this couple came in and sat on the next desk to them.... She said that he sounded just like the guy I had been seeing! "Oh" I said, sounds like him, I will drop him a text which simply said "have a fantastic time on your holiday, where did you book eventually?" A few minutes later my mobile phone rang, it was Charlie "How the f**k did you know I had booked my holiday?" I responded by saying "You would be surprised what I get to know! Why didn't you tell me you had a girlfriend?" At this point I heard a load of what must have been expletives in a very broad Glaswegian accent before he ended the call! It's a good job I couldn't tell what he was saying half the time, he sounded just like Russ Abbott when he does the 'Jimmy' impression!

Isn't it funny how things work out? I never saw his cute Scottish ass again…. Wonder what he is doing now? Probably the same as he did with me but in a different part of the UK!

Murder on the Dance Floor. . . . . . . Nearly!

This is how it started. Upon reflection, what a shamefully pathetic story, and I think I'm reasonably intelligent! good god what was I thinking!!!???

In post-divorce days I arranged to meet through the t'internet a local Manchester club DJ. He was wild and exciting and just what I thought I needed as totally the opposite of my ex husband. He chased me by always playing the songs I liked to dance to and constantly flattering me from his DJ booth (I realised later it wasn't just me he did this to but I was blind and usually blind drunk too)Once he got my number there was no stopping the continuous texts obviously until the early hours and he never put any spaces inbetween his words AND used text speak AND couldn't spell eg: ulokdsogojuslasnite(you looked so gorgeous last night)They were very cryptic texts to unravel but I loved them. I don't recall ever going out anywhere with him(you can so see the signs were staring me in the face!!!) we just carried on partying after hours or I met him at his flat and we'd watch films, talk rubbish and drink. He avoided intimate physical contact and I eventually realised why when one hazy afternoon we got very physical and let's just say his 6ft 3 frame hid a tiny little secret if you know what I mean. I didn't care, he made me laugh and now I had something else to laugh at! Whoever made the statement that "size doesn't matter it's how you use it" DID NOT know what they were talking about!!

One night at the club I was a bit worse for wear on the vodka and my DJ came out of his booth and started slow dancing and smooching with another woman. I was outraged! My friends tried to calm me down but I was having none of it, I was like a woman possessed and I charged across the dance floor tapped him on the shoulder and hit him square on the face with my best right hook that I didn't even know I had, it was the type of club that played vinyl and the song jumped and scratched as the DJ was now flat on the dance floor, his new partner scarpered and my friends quickly lead me away and out saying "Guess that's us barred then"

About 2 days later, surprisingly, Mr DJ called me begging forgiveness and saying he would like to actually get to know me better and lets become an item. I apologised for thumping him and started to even entertain the thought of him as a boyfriend (despite the obvious lying AND lack of presence in the trouser department) I was about to go on a week course in Brighton and so in my naivety suggested he join me, he was on a course in London so I said, "Let's make it romantic and meet at the station" he agreed and the texts continued: "icantw84rwkendinbriteton" "cuatthestatungorjus"

On the train on the way down I changed from my jeans and t-shirt in the toilets into a short dress and stockings and heels and prepared to meet him at the station. The texts stopped at 2am that morning and I just presumed he was busy finding his way from London. I arrived in Brighton at 2pm and no sign, his phone switched off, no texts nothing. I waited until 4pm before realising it must be his revenge for the right hook and I skulked off to my hotel, called my best gay pal Allan (who was the only one who knew what I was up to) and threatened to throw myself off Brighton Pier. He talked me round and kept me sane for the few days I was working there and then met me at the train station when I came home, and we trashed men over a bottle of Pinot. A few weeks later I received a text from a number no longer in my phone memory it said"sozistuduupluvjustnotr eddy4arelatunship"

The wrong number

Another POF encounter! Roland was a large framed guy, 6'2" with shaved head, looked a bit like a thug on his profile picture, however could actually hold a relatively intellectual conversation! He also worked on the railway (what's going on with these railway guys?) so travelled about the country - he was in Coventry at the time and would be working there for a few more weeks until the job in hand had finished. Because of his shift work and location it wasn't that easy to find a suitable time to meet for a drink, and for some reason whenever we did plan to meet I re-arranged on about 3 or 4 occasions. When you have been working all day I didn't seem to have the energy or will to get showered, changed, do hair and nails, which with hindsight must have been a 'sign' of something!

It was a Saturday night and we should have been meeting earlier in the day, however, I decided to put it off so text him to say can we meet the week after? He replied and said that he couldn't as he was going away on holiday and wouldn't be back for three weeks. OK I said, just get in touch when you're back and we can arrange a date and time then and told him to enjoy his holiday. OK he said thanks.

At about 2.30am that night, or Sunday morning, I heard my mobile phone chime to say that I had received a text message. "who the hell is texting me now?" I wondered. I picked up my phone to see that Roland had messaged me and said "Hello my darling, I can't sleep as I can't stop thinking about you! I have been writing my speech and can't w8 for our big day, not long now my love" Oh my, he was going away to get married! The arsehole! I felt so sorry for whoever it was he was going to get married to that's for sure! I text Roland back to say "I really do not want to know, especially at 2.30am that he was writing his bloody wedding speech!" and wished him good luck. A few minutes later another text was received explaining that he was a Best Man at a friends wedding! Yeah right! The first text did NOT read like that at all. I replied and said "The vows he was about to take are completely meaningless you hypocrite" That was that anyway, but couldn't believe that guys actually do these things! "What is going on in the world?" I ask myself quite often!

A few months later, still on POF, a receive a message from someone who looks similar to Roland, but couldn't really tell as a) I had not met him in person before and b) he profile picture was a different one. Carried on chatting to him, and wasn't quite sure if he was Roland, he said his name was Gerald.

After a few weeks of chatting I agreed to meet him one lunch time in a pub. He turned up in a Audi A8, large car, but needed to be to fit him in it! He was a really big guy, not really fat, just big built! He had a shaved head, light blue jeans on, a checked shirt and an imitation plastic leather look jacket which he must have purchased many years ago! We went into the pub, got a drink and sat down, we started chatting and as he was answering my questions and telling me about himself I realised that there were too many coincidences for him not to be Roland!! "Gerald my arse" I thought, this HAS to be Roland.

Half an hour later he slopes off to the gents, so I text him from where I was sat "Don't be long Roland will you?" He emerged from the gents with a rather sheepish look on his face and said "well, if I had told you who I was you wouldn't have met me would you?" "You're damn right" and went on to ask him what happened on his wedding day - did he still make those vows? He told me that he didn't go through with the ceremony and is now single - he said that it wasn't right! I didn't ask any more, made a sharp exit and told him not to contact me again - as I said before....... Arsehole!

From Leicester with Veg!
(not from Russia with Love)

Well hello!! I thought as I received an email from this rather sexy, gorgeous looking Italian….. On his profile he said he was 6'1" tall, slim, long dark shoulder length wavy hair (a bit like a footballer's hair style) brown eyes, perfect teeth and spoke with a very sexy Italian accent!! Wow, my boat has come in I think….. At last!!

We chatted for about 4 weeks via email, Instant Messaging on the dating site we were on, text messages and phone calls - he was very romantic, passionate and intense about everything he did. He lived in Leicester, a few hours drive away from me, living in a large house overlooking a lake apparently - well one day hopefully I may find out for real! Well I didn't have to wait for long, Demitri invited me over the following weekend to spend some quality time with him. He was 38 years old and never married, no bambinos so he was free as a bird!! He owned his own business which was a driving school and employed a few qualified drivers - he was very busy and was obviously successful at what he did.

So, on this particular Friday afternoon after work, I packed my overnight case (gym bag actually, but overnight case sounded more romantic!) showered, did my hair and made sure my make-up was perfect. Piled into my car and headed for the motorway network via a petrol station to fill up!! Gosh, my stomach was doing somersaults at the thought of meeting this most gorgeous Italian guy........ I was REALLY looking forward to meeting him after all this time! (Not long I know relatively speaking but it felt like it had been forever!) Off I set into the sunset (rain and cloud actually) and headed due south on my 3 hour journey hoping there was a pot of gold to be found at the end of this t'internet rainbow!!

After a 3.5 hours drive, my Satnav eventually directed me to this detached 4 bedroom house set in its own grounds with the back garden sloping down to the edge of this large lake which was inhabited with swans, ducks and those little black birds with a white beak! (I can't remember what they're called but I'm sure you know what I'm on about!) The house must have been built in the early 20th Century (gosh, I sound like an antiques road show bod!!) given its deep red brick and style. As I drove onto the newly paved driveway, a black cat shot out of the front door as it gently opened to reveal this Italian god-like illusion stood watching me park my car. (OMG I must have been dreaming... this felt sooooo surreal!! As I attempted to extract myself from my car in a lady-like manner Dimitri very coolly walked towards me – he was wearing a delicate pink polo shirt and three quarter length light blue denim jeans and a pair of flip-flops. Wow, how gorgeous did he look, THE man of my dreams! He gently put his arms around me, looked deep into my eyes, said 'hi beautiful' obviously using his stunning Italian accent!! My knees turned to jelly as he kissed me softly for a few seconds on my lips...... 'That's it.' I said to myself, 'I never want to be anywhere else, HE IS my man and I will be trying everything within my power to win his love and we can live happily ever after, and who knows we could have a bambino or two as I was still young enough! How stunning looking would our kids be.....?'

My daydreaming abruptly came to an end when I hear this voice asking me for my keys so he could get my bag out of the boot. I quickly responded and before I knew it, we were both naked on a most stunning white leather corner sofa! I have to say it IS true what they say about Italian Stallions!!! Phew!! He was AMAZING! I had never seen a six pack like that before in action...... I could be lost for words, but as ever I'm not!! If I liken him to a stallion then the words I would use to describe him would be: Dark, Strong, Mysterious, Deep, Muscular, Intense, Sensuous, Proud and lots of stamina!! Oh my, this weekend is certainly going to be a turning point in my life....

Given that food plays a significant part in any Italians life, it wouldn't surprise you to say that most of the weekend was spent either cooking, eating, drinking, walking and any other words you can think of ending in 'ing' (yes the one beginning with F too!!) oh and making love, Italians do both I found out!! I was in heaven, on the Sunday before I returned home, we spent the afternoon sunbathing in the back garden, listening to the birds on the lake, chill-out music (Ibiza) kissing, holding hands and just sinking into each other!! The thought of leaving him was awful, I really did not want to go back home!! Oh well, I thought, I will be seeing him again in a couple of weeks as he had invited me back over to his place. It was difficult for him to come to mine at weekends due to his business as there was a lot of demand at the weekend for driving lessons, however, he did say that he would be able to come over to mine in a month or so when he had a relatively quiet weekend.

My return visit to see Dimitri two weeks later was just as fantastic and magical, nothing had changed and it was very clear that he had really missed me. He was like my shadow and said he couldn't bear to be without me..... needless to say we never ventured out of the house for long for a lazy walk on the Saturday morning to the local shops for some fresh fruit and vegetables and of course stock up on the bubbly!! (Champagne). I didn't realise until I got home on the Sunday that I had been driving for about 3 hours with a smile on my face….. I must have fallen for this guy!! Oh Dear, already, I had told myself previously that I must remain in control of my emotions!! 'How do you do that then when you heart has fallen for someone?' I wondered….. do people exist in a state of denial?

Another 3 weeks passed very slowly, and all I could think about was when I was next going to see Dimitri – eventually the day arrived and he text me to tell me he was setting out to my place and that he had been shopping and would cook dinner for us when he arrived. Fantastic I thought, it doesn't get any better than this does it?

A few hours later he arrived and parked his car (with the name of his driving school plastered all over it including one of those square signs on the roof so everyone in the neighbourhood could see who I had staying with me! In fact, if they were that way inclined they could have called him on his mobile number which was obviously well advertised at the top of his car!!) on the road in the front of my house. He emerged with bags full of shopping containing mostly fresh vegetables, dairy products, fresh herbs and some fresh chicken.

A gave Dimitri a huge hug and some kisses as he came through the front door before he could even put any bags down!! Bless him I thought, I mustn't smother him just yet…..;-) We both went into the kitchen, and chatted for a while about the days events before I went to get a shower and freshen up for the evening whilst he prepared all the vegetables. When I came back down from the bathroom he was still carefully and with precision chopping the peppers, tomatoes, courgettes, garlic, herbs and seasoning which he was about to drizzle (I love that word, Drizzle!) in olive oil, sprinkle (let me say that again, Sprinkle!) with the finely chopped herbs before placing in the oven to gently roast.

As Dimitri closed the oven, he asked me if there was a local shop where he could purchase a bottle of wine and a mobile top-up card? Yes, I replied there is a 'Tesco Express around the corner' and duly pointed him in the right direction. As I watched him drive down the road, I thought it was rather strange to be going out to purchase more stuff when he had already been shopping!! Wouldn't you have thought that he would have purchased the wine and mobile top-up phone all at the same time? Oh well, I thought, he must have just forgotten.

Whilst he was gone I set the dining room table, turned down the lights and lit a few candles to generate the right mood for when he came back. Once I had done this (which took about 10 minutes) I sat down and opened a bottle of red wine, poured a small glass and chilled listening to some music for a short while before embarking on another raunchy romantic evening with my Italian Stallion.

After about 10 minutes I started to wonder whether he had got lost as the shop was only around the corner, maybe it's busy and there is a queue, as sometimes on a Friday evening this can be the case. I carried on chilling, another 10 minutes passed, and another, and another...... an hour later there was still no sign!! I felt my stomach turn over and felt rather nauseous, oh no, not again, what has gone wrong now? I tried his mobile phone which rang out and just went to the answer phone.... I started to panic and wonder whether he had been in an accident or not. I immediately put on my boots and walked around to the shop which was about a 10 minute walk away(couldn't drive as I had had a couple of glasses of vino by then!). As I turned the corner from which point you could see the shop I braced myself as I had visualised some sort of pile-up…….. No! nothing there, all was 'business as usual' with people coming and going. I felt rather ill, he was nowhere in sight. Reality suddenly hit…… HE had done a runner!! I stood there for a few seconds trying very hard to consciously stop any tears emerging, before turning around and making my way back home!! I felt lost and gutted….. What had happened? We were so happy together……. I just couldn't make sense of this!!!

Needless to say, I NEVER saw Dimitri again – I tried to ring him on a number of occasions, however no response……. So to this day, I never saw or heard from him again!!! ANOTHER strange encounter……..!!!!

The Lake District Lover

Not the type of guy I would normally go for, a 6"1' tall slim build, a keep fit fanatic with a shaved head. His name was Paul, an ex-police officer (retired now) who had lost his wife a few years ago through the dreaded "C" word - Cancer!

I had also lost my husband to cancer several years before who was more like an Italian guy, shorter, darker and dark hair, oh and a little plumper!! So total opposites really – but hey - variety is the spice of life!!

We had been chatting for several weeks initially we had a lot in common having both lost partners but as the weeks went on we developed a very close friendship through email text and eventually telephone - we would chat online for at least an hour every night and then once his children had gone to bed - he had teenagers mine were older and married - we would talk on the phone for a further hour. We both said we could not believe how close you could become to someone you had not even met!

We lived over 150 miles apart and I was worried how a relationship could work over such a distance but Paul assured me it could and planned to come to visit me in a month's time when he could arrange for the children to be looked after for a few days - it seemed ages away and we were both desperate to meet so I suggested I went up to meet him, he said he could arrange for the children to be looked after overnight and we made plans for the weekend. I asked him to find me a cheap hotel - near enough to where he lived so we could meet but far enough to be safe so the children would not find out - we had both agreed it was too early to tell them.

The day before I was due to go up he called me and said he had booked a 5* hotel on the beach of one of the lakes so we could take a stroll along the waterfront before dinner - I had said in my profile that my ideal date was a walk on the beach! He also asked what my favourite champagne was - my god I've found myself a real romantic! My ideal man!! We spent an idyllic two days together - holding hands, kissing, cuddling, making love and making me feel like I was the ONLY woman on the planet!!! (shouldn't that be how its supposed to be?) Paul was just as I had expected and he said he felt the same, by the time I left to travel back home, he said those three little words "I love you" and I had reciprocated. My heart was alive again!! I just couldn't believe what was happening to me, especially after all the hurt and pain I had gone through when I lost my husband, my soul mate!! I NEVER thought I would be as happy again, I was wrong!! I WAS happy again.. The happiest woman on earth!!

On my way home he text me "come back I miss you already" - I had only travelled 5 miles down the road when I received this….. I was glowing!!! I was no longer a bird with wounded wings… my spirit was flying free again!!! (words from one of my fave dance tunes!) When I got home Paul sent me an e mail saying he had put a note on his profile saying he had found his 'soul mate'. We continued to text and call daily and he said he could not wait to come down and visit me at the end of the month - but that was 4 weeks away, his birthday was in two weeks so I went to visit him again just for the day, again a wonderful, magical day. When we spoke that night he said his son had said that Paul's bed had smelt 'strangely nice'- which of course was my perfume! He told me he loved me and wanted to spend the rest of his life with me - I was unsure about the distance but he said we could make it work - I was reassured once again by Paul, who I was hoping to be my future husband!! I prayed every night that this would be the case and we would live happily ever after!! Just like they do in the Walt Disney films!

We continued our chatting on line and late night conversations however over the next two weeks they became less frequent - I could not call him because of the children and so I would wait for him to call when I knew it was convenient for him, however gradually they were getting less frequent. Paul would explain to me the next day that he was sorry he had not phoned but that he was tired and had fallen asleep. He told me he was looking forward to coming down the following week and I had booked the days off work, I had also booked the opera as a birthday treat as he had said he loved the opera - not really my scene but I was willing to try it!

The day before he was due to come down I got a text from Paul saying that he wasn't feeling too good and was going to see his GP. He called me that night and said he would not be able to come down as the doctor had booked him in for several tests at the hospital on the Friday including a brain scan to check things out, apparently he had been suffering with headaches and migraines just lately. He told me he was scared as it was all so quick! I didn't hear from him for the rest of the week and kept texting and phoning him to see if he wanted me to go with him - he said a friend was going with him and he would not put me through the trauma of hospitals again - when I asked what he meant he said I had been through this with my husband and he refused to put me through it all again - they thought he had a brain tumour which is ironically what my husband had died from some years earlier!!! My heart sank.... How can this be? Why should this be happening now especially now we had found each other?!!? Let's not jump to conclusions too quickly and wait and see what the results say! I took a deep breath but still kept praying every night for him!!

Paul told me he went for this scan, which happened very quickly, the only contact I had from him was to tell me it wasn't a brain tumour but something very similar which would need surgery and a long recovery time. I was gutted, as I had started to fall head over heels in love with this guy and thought he felt the same way too!!! I kept texting him, calling him now and again to see how he was and to see if there was anything I could do - I desperately wanted to be there for him and support him through this, however he just completely ignored me - something I found very difficult to understand. The responses from him were few and far between and didn't say much at all, just one or two words... "tired" etc, he never asked again how I was which was very hard to deal with as not long ago we were like two long term lovers who had the rest of our lives to enjoy together! I felt ill, sick to the bone, I couldn't think of anything else apart from him and the suffering/stressful time he must be going through bearing in mind he had also lost his wife to cancer a few years ago and had two young children to consider. My heart was near to breaking point, so in the end I just had to ring him to see what was going on. Guess what, no answer! I kept trying to get in touch with him, I was out of my mind with worry and concern and hurt! I couldn't go back to the lakes as his 2 sons still lived with him, who did not know of my existence, so that wasn't a realistic option really! Then one morning I awoke very early for some reason, and checking my e mails saw that I had a couple of messages - I looked to see who they were from and yes, one of them was from Paul, my heart flipped over as though I was on "The Big One" at Blackpool pleasure beach! I held my breath as I clicked on the 'select' button on the handset.... "Hi babes, I have not been in contact with you, it's been difficult for me" that was it! No explanation! No apology! I wrote back asking what was happening, was he ok, but no reply.

A few days later I received another email from Paul - this time just a joke email and he sent a number of these over the next few days! When I looked at the other recipients I saw there was someone new to his mailing list called Cheryl who was obviously from a dating site given the name of her email address!! I couldn't resist checking her profile out on the dating site.... and when I went on to it she had written a message saying 'where has my soul mate gone - I want him back'!

This left me with many unanswered questions - Was this a coincidence? Or had he been stringing us both along! Was he a serial heart breaker or the genuinely nice guy I had thought he was with bad luck that he fell ill just as we had found each other?

I guess I will never know but I have learnt an important lesson from this - t'internet dating is good fun as long as you stay in control and use the men as much as they use you - which until this guy I had done and had some real fun!!! But be very cautious if you decide to let your heart get involved ladies as you are likely to get it broken! So back to the drawing board and look for more fun with no strings this time............well maybe!! Or is it Friends With Benefits now? (FWB)

BIGMAC – large or extra-large!?!

Well, this guy had been hassling me for about 3 months on this particular website. I had chatted with him using IM on the odd occasion but mostly the exchange had been via emails through the website. Some of his emails were very lengthy and made reference to Shakespeare and other poems which were rather deep and meaningful!!

On his profile he had uploaded a number of pictures of himself dressed in combat gear, the odd pose whilst doing some sort of martial arts with a red bandana around his head and one with a pair of combat trousers on and nothing at the top exposing his muscular torso!! He had dark hair which had done a vanishing act in the middle which left him with 2 dark tufts on each side of his head (much like a baby blackbird or thrush when their newly grown feathers protruding out of the top of their cute little heads!) Mmmmm, I thought I would prefer to meet someone with hair all over, but can't be fussy at my age hey!! As long as he keeps it short I could cope with that, and at least he has teeth from what I can see from his pics!!

Dee (Derek) described himself as 6'4", Ex-special forces, divorced, 2 boys from his previous marriage and looking for a long term, serious relationship with a special lady!! So eventually after he had consistently tried to grab my attention, I thought that I would give him my contact number as he had been persistent, he sounded fun with a good sense of humour and wanted a long term relationship – we exchanged mobile numbers.

Over the next few days the text messages and phone calls came thick and fast! He told me he wasn't working at the time as he was off sick with a hand injury, but then let it slip that he was helping his mate out with his work whilst he was off!!! "Mmmm, dodgy" I thought!! Every few hours I would receive another text which was very romantic and thoughtful. In the evenings he would be very keen to call me and have a 'real' voice to voice conversation which was fine and a good opportunity to get to know him better!! Well, I certainly did that!!! We had planned to meet for dinner in a couple of weeks at a location half way between where we both lived. I have to say I was a bit apprehensive about meeting him as he said that if we did get on then he would book a hotel room for the weekend and we could really get to know each other.........! I left that comment hanging in the air and didn't respond at the time! So over the next couple of weeks up until the day before we were due to meet, we maintained contact on a regular daily basis and oh boy, all I can say is that he was very forthcoming and didn't hold ANYTHING back.....

I found out over those 2 weeks about his 'Flag Pole'..... yes you guessed it he was referring to his 10" family jewels of which he was very proud and went on to tell me about this date he had been on a few weeks ago. Apparently he had gone out with this gorgeous looking lady commando style, and because he was so turned on by her that he had no control over the situation as he walked into a pub with her which caused a lot of 'eye traffic' around the crotch of his trousers!!! Well, I asked myself… why the hell did I want to know about that? Answer…. I didn't!!

He also went on to inform me that he had killed more men than most when he was in the Special Forces and in order to take early leave and remain financially comfortable he spent a number of months as a male escort!! This particular escort agency was apparently a 'high class' one which meant that the main role for the guys was NOT sex!! Well, from what Dee said I think he got rather mixed up!! He had decided that if he did fancy any of the ladies he escorted they were "avin it whether they liked it or not" and in fact "he didn't mind if he paid them at the end of the night instead of them paying him"!!! Oh dear, my impression of this guy was rapidly going downhill!!

When I asked him about the type of woman he was looking for his first response was that he was ONLY interested in ladies over the age of 35. He went on to tell me that he had slept with 7 women in total under the age of 30 and they were all terrible in bed!! They all had fantastic bodies but didn't know what to do with them!!

Towards the end of the second week he confirmed that he was in fact looking for a new Mrs MacDonald and explained that he felt that I was different from all the other slappers on the websites and that he had developed real feelings for me and couldn't wait to meet me so we could start our lives together. On this same day he proposed to me over the phone 4 times and this was before we had even met!! What on earth was going on? Do guys not understand the meaning of a proposal? Obviously not!!

I thought that I would play the game with him and informed him the day before we were to meet for dinner that I had been looking at engagement rings and had seen one that I really loved!! "Fantastic he said" all we need to do now is find out the size of your finger and I will be able to slip it on...... he was very keen to get married that year!!

We carried on chatting and said that we would speak the next day to confirm dinner arrangements....... Well, guess what? I never heard from him again even though I did send him a text asking him if he had changed his mind!!

Tell me, why on earth should a guy enact a charade like that after spending 3 months trying to grab my attention; inform me of the size of his family jewels; propose; arrange dinner; and then f**k off? It's all a game, it must be? Is this where male egos come into play?

The wrong size

Graham was about 5'10", medium build, divorced, had children in their early 20's and was looking for a long term relationship.

When I first met him I was taken aback by how blue and sparkly his eyes were and that his little goatee, which was perfectly trimmed gave him a rather distinguished look. When we first spoke on the phone he came across as very well spoken, with rather a deep but gentle voice.

It became clear very early on that he liked the finer things in life and **had** lived in a very lush detached house in an area renowned for where footballers with huge salaries lived. After chatting for a week or so over the phone we made arrangements to go for a bite to eat in an area with posh restaurants and wine bars, "How nice" I thought, finally I get to meet a well-spoken gentleman who prefers the finer things in life….. I hope he considers me to be one of the finer things in his life….. let's wait and see hey?

When making arrangements to meet for the first time, he informed me that he would be in this posh Italian restaurant and would be at the bar….. sounded like this was his local and he would know everyone in there! Fine, I thought, perhaps I would get to meet a few of his friends and would also prove that he had nothing to hide ie wasn't married or in a long term relationship already!!

At that time of year the nights were drawing in which meant that I would have to find my way in the dark, not a problem I thought and off I went on my little adventure for the evening, but secretly hoping that this would be the start of a long term adventure with a posh guy!! As I walked up to the restaurant I noticed that my first obstacle was a rather steep, wet and slippery set of stairs up to the bar/restaurant area. I noticed Graham sat strategically placed at the bar so he could see everyone entering or leaving the restaurant...... "No pressure" I thought to myself as I concentrated on the stairs making sure that I didn't catch my stiletto heels on anything and end up 'ass over tit' and make a huge embarrassing scene!! As I got to the top of the stairs I was greeted by a warm and welcoming smile and 2 kisses, 1 on each cheek, you know, how the French or Italians greet each other!!

Over the next few hours we enjoyed a really nice Italian meal with a couple of glasses of wine with lots of conversation about life, work, family and what our journey had been like through life. When the bill came Graham very quickly accepted my offer to pay 50% (I don't like to assume that the guy always pays on a first date!). We continued to see each other for a few months and each time he always insisted on sorting out a 'kitty' for drinks and food which was sort of off-putting ie taking away any romance or the feeling that you are being wined and dined!! Oh well, both of us work and going 50/50 isn't really a bad thing...... is it?

For the first weekend we decided to spend together ie spending the night together, Graham suggested that we go out to "Passage to India" an Indian restaurant in the village where he lives (by this time I hadn't been to his pad, which I understood to be a Georgian property where he rented the ground floor flat. "OK" I said, "sounds like a plan to me!" Needless to say the Saturday was spent de-fluffing, doing nails and deciding what to wear - especially on the underwear front - first impressions and all that! I arrived at Grahams pad at about 7.30ish after a 45 minute drive up the motorway, so not far to drive really. I didn't get invited in at that point as Graham was chomping at the bit for his Indian meal, as such I was very quickly greeted at the door and informed that I could get my things out of the car when we got back!! Again, we had a very pleasant evening, during which we topped up the 'kitty' twice as the wine was flowing rather well!! It was about midnight when we walked back to his pad, hand in hand which was rather nice as it had been a long time since I had had any physical contact with a male!! Needless to say we didn't make the bedroom until the early hours in the morning due to the fact that 'lust' had taken over our brains as we sat on the sofa watching the golf highlights!!! As we got down to 'it' I was rather taken aback by the size of his 'manhood'…….. 'it' was TINY!!!! No word of a lie it must have been about 4 inches long and the girth of a dinner candle!!! WHAT a disappointment…… I didn't realise that I had actually 'started the race' until his rather loud expressions (and hell they were loud! Good job the brick walls were the old type and kept sound in!!) of pleasure demonstrated to me that he had already crossed the finish line!!! How good was that? NOT!!! As Graham made himself decent again I couldn't help but take a glance at this hands….. Yes his fingers were tiny!!! More evidence to show that there is a correlation between the size of men's hands and their manhood!!! So ladies, or gents, lesson is to take a good look at their hands before you decide to get intimate with your partner…. Savloy or Cocktail Sausage?……….. Savloy EVERY time for me!!!!

The other thing I hadn't noticed either until we were on our way to bed that we had had an audience! A tank full of Piranha's which Graham quickly fed with locusts as he had forgotten o feed them that day as he had been busy playing golf!!

A few months later we were out again in the village where he lived. We ended up in this Spanish tapas bar which had live music on and was very busy….. Fab atmosphere! Anyway, it was getting on for throwing out time when Graham put his arm around my waste (we were stood at the bar) pulled me close to him and said "take a look in the mirror" (a huge mirror which ran the length of the bar wall where the optics were fixed) I looked across the bar and looked in the mirror….. Yes, it was our reflection….. Before I could say anything Graham said to me "what a good looking couple we are"…….. awwww, how nice is that?………. He very quickly went on to say…… "if you were a size 10 I would fall in love with you" WHAT??!!!???? I thought to myself…… you cheeky superficial B*****d!!! After all this time he decides to say that!!! Immediately I thought about telling him that I would fall in love with him if he had an extension in his basement!! I didn't however share that thought with him as I had been drinking and needed somewhere to stay for the night!! I never said a word and carried on as normal (well, apart from the sex bit!). That night we just went straight to sleep and I left fairly early the next morning as he was playing golf again!!!

Needless to say, yet another let down!!! I don't blame Kevin and Perry for going LARGE in Ibiza!!! Small just won't do!!!

"I give up!" ☹

Why 'I' Mon!

I got chatting to this guy Gary on Smooch.com, he was 8 years younger than me, never been married and had one daughter aged 7 who he saw every other weekend. He lived with his parents in Newcastle-upon-Tyne, owned a flat but rented it out!! Didn't really find out why this was the case even though I did ask!! He worked in the security industry and was looking for a long term relationship with preferably an older woman...... Great!! Just what I was looking for. I did sort of wonder about the distance between us as it was a 4 hour journey to see each other, but hey, if you find your soul mate and fall in love, then distance isn't an obstacle is it?!!

We had been in contact for about 3 months before we made arrangements for him to come over to mine for the weekend. He was a really nice guy, he used to text me all the time to see how I was, he would ring me most days and vice versa so by the time we got to meet up we didn't feel like complete strangers. On this particular weekend Gary said he would be leaving his home at about 9am on the Saturday morning so should be with me at 1ish dependent upon traffic and weather. It was the autumn time so plenty of rain as you would expect in the UK, and especially the North East. He said that he didn't have a car of his own and was able to use his works van for personal reasons which wasn't a problem as we had agreed to book a taxi later to take us out into town. I had booked a table at an Italian restaurant which was in the city centre near to the pubs and clubs so we would have a choice of venues to go to dependent upon the mood!!

All morning I did housework so the house was presentable and tidy when he arrived - so all the big knickers had to be removed from radiators and put back in the wash basket for the weekend!! At 1pm exactly I received a text from Gary to tell me he wasn't far away from me and explained that he was on a pub car park, The George which was just around the corner from me. I called him straight away on his mobile to tell him that I would make my way to the car park and meet him there. I dived into my car and headed in his direction….. Ooooer!! Butterflies sure were fluttering…. I do hope that we hit it off……..!!!

Two minutes late I arrived on the car park to see this white Vauxhall van with the roof rack piled high with aluminium ladders - that has to be him then. I drove to the distant corner where he was parked and pulled up so our drivers windows were parallel with each other. We both smiled at each other, he stayed in his car with the window wound down and I got out. He never made a move to get out of his car so I asked him for a hug!! After all this time surely this would be the first thing he wanted to do!! Perhaps he is a bit shy now we have actually met!! He got out of his van and gave me a hug… no kisses, just a hug which is fine!!! He was wearing a white T-shirt, imitation leather jacket, dark blue jeans and white trainers…… He did explain later that he had bought his best shoes with him that had cost him £80 a few years ago!!! It sounded then that he didn't really spend much money on himself…. Well, at least he had a decent pair of shoes and wasn't going to go out with his white trainers on!! Phew!!! We both got back into our cars and Gary followed me back to my place. He managed to find a car parking space on the street which was a few doors down which was a good thing so the nosey neighbours couldn't see what was happening in my life at this time!!

I noticed as he walked towards me that he was carrying a Next carrier bag and wondered if he had decided to bring me a gift or something...... WRONG!! This was his environmentally friendly weekend away travel case......!!! He mustn't have much in it as it was one of the smaller carrier bags. When we got into mine and I put the kettle on to make a nice cup of tea!!! (no bubbly then just yet!), he immediately 'unpacked' his carrier bag and at the same time said out loud what each item was. He took out a checked shirt which was still on the hanger and hung it onto a wall light fitting, took out his shoes which were nice, a pair of socks and a pair of boxers which he neatly placed under the shirt hanging on the wall. "Oh no" he said suddenly, I have forgotten my toothbrush….. "We can get one when we go shopping" I replied as this is what we had arranged to do on the Saturday afternoon before going out in the evening.

Half an hour after Gary arrived we both piled into my car and off we went shopping - he said that he wanted a pair of jeans if he saw a pair he liked and of course a tooth brush. We spent about 3 hours in town and bought….. Yes you guessed it….. A TOOTH BRUSH that was on offer for 38 pence from Superdrug!! Last of the big spenders hey!! Time was ticking on and I was getting fed up of selecting jeans off the rails and asking him if he liked them….. Out of all the jeans he didn't like any of them as they had to be of a certain cut and if they weren't they would look daft as he was pigeon toed and his knees were not where they were supposed to be!! OK, I thought, we all have imperfections, as long as he can walk in a straight line more or less then that's a bonus!! As we walked back to the car I did notice that he walked slightly odd but that was OK…. I also noticed that he didn't want to hold hands or make any physical contact with me which made me feel rather uneasy!! As we had been walking around the shops every now and again I would touch him on his arm or give him a peck on his cheek but never got anything back….. Mmmmm, I wondered, perhaps he doesn't like me after meeting me. Well, I suppose he had a choice, he could stay or disappear when we get back to mine, no doubt I will find out soon!!

When we got back to mine I said that I would go and get ready soon and we could have a beer or glass of wine whilst we got ready if he wanted. Yes, a beer would be nice. As I went to get the drinks Gary asked me if I would take his shirt upstairs when I went to get ready!! Sure, I said, but also thought this was a rather strange thing to ask me to do when he would be going to get ready anyway!! Perhaps he was testing out how accommodating I was!!! Anyway, I did forget to take his shirt upstairs with me so he had to carry it up when it was his turn to get ready!! (I must have been on my own for too long!!)

It was 7.30 Saturday in the evening and we were waiting for the taxi to arrive so in between polite conversation I kept looking out of the window to check so we didn't keep the driver waiting. To my horror a 12 seater mini bus turned up!! We quickly got into the mini bus and sat next to each other…… I decided to hold his hand otherwise there would be no physical contact at all!! The taxi driver must have been dragged out of a retirement home for the evening as he must have driven at an average speed of 10 miles per hour!!! He was horrendous and kept missing the gears which either nearly killed the engine or nearly killed us as we were thrown forwards each time he put the vehicle into 2nd gear instead of 4th!!!! We felt rather sea sick by the time we arrived but it did break the ice a bit as we both laughed our heads off when he eventually dropped us outside the restaurant.

The Italian meal was very nice, eventually!!! after I had asked to move tables further away from the till where everyone kept coming to pay - it was a bit like Euston station on Friday. I did get the impression that Gary had been a bit embarrassed about me asking to change tables... perhaps he was rather a shy guy!! Or was I just a bit more assertive than other women he had been out with!!!

The evening was OK, nothing earth shattering! No dance floor was involved or loud music as he didn't dance because of his knees!! So I ended up just sort of dancing on the spot in a couple of the bars we went into!!! There wasn't much physical contact apart from a snog or two when we got back and had gone to bed! Gary kept his tartan boxers on and his T-shirt and I put my pj's on. We were like a married couple or something!! There was obviously something wrong but I couldn't quite work it out........ I just came to the conclusion that he was either very shy or just didn't fancy me!!

In the morning he had obviously woken up rather erect (even though he was still wearing his tartan boxer shorts I could tell!) and after a couple of kisses excused himself as he rushed to the bathroom before his 'out of control' family jewels 'twinkled' when they were not supposed to 'twinkle'! Oh dear, how embarrassing for him! Whilst he was in the bathroom I decided to get up, get dressed and go and make a cup of tea. Gary came down 10 minutes later also dressed. I gave him his tea and asked him if he would like some breakfast. He told me he didn't normally eat breakfast but would have a piece of toast with me. I made him his toast and asked him if would like marmalade on it.... He said he would try it but had never had marmalade before......... He really had led a sheltered life hadn't he!!!??? Bless him!

Gary had his slice of toast before settling down to watch a bit of sports news before telling me in order to get home ready to watch the F1 racing at 1.00pm he would have to leave at 10.30 at the latest. Oh right, OK, I understand, he couldn't wait to get away from me..... Oh well, another failure!!! I never said anything apart from drive carefully when he left the house and to let me know when he gets home. Gary said goodbye...... and nothing else at all!! Ie I don't want to see you again, or indeed, when are we going to see each other again..... How strange I thought!!

A few hours later he text me to tell me he had arrived back home safely..... And that was it for a few weeks and then suddenly he text me to ask me when we could go out again... .....I was confused dot com!!

Eventually via text messages he told me that he absolutely fancied the pants off me but couldn't show his feelings as he would have got carried away too quickly in terms of a relationship with me!!! He did admit to being distant with me but would love to see me again and would love to start a long term relationship!!!! Why couldn't he just be himself then when we did meet? I found his behaviour rather strange and therefore I declined to meet with him again!

Another wrong number

I was just in the process of cleaning out my car when a call came through on my mobile from a mobile number I didn't recognise. I had recently given my number out to this guy on t'internet so assumed it would be him!! As I answered I heard this very husky, deep cockney accent...... 'phew' whoever it was immediately made my knees go weak!! Gosh, what was that all about? After he had asked for this person (which wasn't me!) he apologised and explained that the number he rang used to be his ex-girlfriends number (yes, I had just been given a new number from Vodaphone as I had changed provider a few days earlier). Ian and I got chatting and flirting and ended up texting each other and speaking rather regularly on the phone. After about a month or so it was clear that there was definitely chemistry between us and we both agreed that we would love to meet for real as we were both looking for long term commitment!! Fantastic, at last, someone who did want to commit to just one lady, and given his personality and beliefs you could tell that you would be 'numbero uno' on his list of priorities.

Ian lived on his own in a flat north of London, smoked but was trying to give up, loved R&B music and was a roof tiler!!! Well, someone has to, it's a very important job!! He had explained to me that his friends thought he looked a lot like crocodile Dundee, tall, slim, blonde hair with a cheeky dimple in his chin!! I would say that this was an accurate description of Ian as I saw him standing on the railway platform waiting for me to arrive!!! Yikes, what WAS I doing? Oh well, I was here now and if I wanted to change my mind I could at any time!!! He seemed like a really genuine down to earth, hard-working guy!! I carefully stepped off the train ie making sure my heels didn't get stuck on anything they shouldn't have done!! He walked up to me and said "Wow baby, you are stunning, you look gorgeous, how are you?" all in one breath I think!! I answered and off we went to get into his car, a Vauxhall saloon of some description to go back to his flat for something to eat. Ian had done all the food shopping and was going to cook for me…. He had also spent 3 weeks painting his flat, something he said he had NEVER done before!! Gosh, I felt honoured!!! This down to earth guy had put every ounce of effort into my visit and wanted everything to be perfect!!! The weekend was great, we went into London shopping, ambled through a food market by the thames river where we grabbed something to eat and every now and again snatched a kiss off each other!! It was rather romantic I have to say, he was very touchy feely and showed that he really wanted a long term relationship with me…… At this point I tried to envisage Ian back at my place and mixing with my friends and family… It wasn't going to happen was it!!

It would have been a bit like the stable boy and the lady of the manor….. He had a bit of an 'all guns firing' personality if someone upset him!! (I found this out when he lost the plot with someone when we were queuing up for a boat ride! - needless to say we were nearly thrown out of the queue!!) He did have a few rough edges so to speak and I didn't think I had a nail file big enough to file them off!!

After a really nice weekend together we both said that we had different lives and that it would be a little like 'Upstairs, Downstairs' if we did ever get together…. So for the sake of keeping the class thing in tact and not creating unnecessary tension for us both, we decided not to take the relationship any further and wished each other good luck for our future lives!! Shame, he was a nice guy with a big heart and I know I would have been the centre of his life!!!

Blind Date

After chatting for a few weeks on AOL I met Mike for the first time in the flesh on a charity run, he kept pace with me on the gruelling 10k around the city centre. He kept singing silly songs to distract from our aching legs when running and making flattering comments about my behind.

As we were in no fit state to be swapping phone numbers at the finishing line I told him to contact me by email and gave him my work email address. Mike called me the following week and we arranged to meet up at his seaside flat one lovely summers evening. He lived in a gorgeous old house converted into flats, overlooking the beach where the tide never came in. He suggested we went for a walk and then a drink in his local pub. Mike was about 6'0" tall, very slim, silver hair, mid-40s, a rather large pointed nose (skinny one though) I thought he was a bit quirky but seemed good amusing company when to get to know his sense of humour!.

He gave me his address so I could travel to the coast for a certain time so we could watch the sunset go down over the sea before we went out for a romantic evening meal at this local pub/restaurant! When I arrived he quickly opened the front door and gave me a full on kiss which suggested that there was a bit of a spark between us. He told me he was a part-time cameraman for a local TV company and would I mind if he brought his hand-held camera to the beach to film the sunset? "What a romantic" I thought, "of course, no problem with me!"

As we walked down to the beach we chatted like old friends and laughed so much about the run we had both been in and taking the 'micky' out of the more colourful characters who had been there. He had a funny way of looking at things and it amused me greatly. He turned on his camera and started to film the sunset with a running commentary which got a tad stranger by the minute. Suddenly the amusement I felt before in his conversation melted away pretty fast as he started being racist, fattist, mysogynistic and just downright insulting about the people walking on the beach in his running commentary as he filmed. He then turned the camera on to me and as I walked on started to be extremely suggestive in a creepy way about me. The final straw came when he kept the camera in his hand and filmed as he grabbed and kissed me with full on tongues pulling away to keep his commentary going commenting on the stirring in his loins!!!

At this point it was beyond a joke, Jeremy Beadle wouldn't have taken it this far, I grabbed his camera and ran stopping only outside the beautiful old house to press rewind and delete and then to the same to my date as I left the camera outside and sped off in my car. Good job this didn't end up on Youtube eh?

Corked and Confused

Now I remember Him. Another Mike though (mike's and John's feature a lot in my love life) my friend's actually named them by year as in: John 2000 , John 20002. Mike 1986 and so on!

After having a few recent disastrous meetings with guys off the internet I decided that I was going to have a night out with my friends clubbing, you know one of those I'm going to snog as many men as I can nights… I met him in a bit of a seedy nightclub (the type where your feet stick to the carpet!) at the end of the night, and I was proper drunk!!!. Those were the days eh? needless to say I was younger and on a mission! I couldn't behave like that in my 40s now could I?

We arranged to meet at a pub the following weekend so all week I was really excited and looking forward to meeting him again!! I thought he was good looking, 6'2" tall, mixed race, his mother was Carribean and his father English, he was a really sweet guy. But almost too sweet. He called me by my name every 5 minutes which really started to annoy me and he was also a bit dim, the drunken night meant I had failed to notice how dumb he was, he could just about string together 2 sentences! Things started to look up when after a couple of drinks he suggested going back to his for a bottle of champagne! Great I might just have a fun one night stand here I thought. We got back to "his" . It was a studenty styled house that smelt of damp and he showed me

74

up to his attic room which was neat and that's about all I can say about it. He disappeared and came back with 2 tumblers and yes it was real champagne, not the charleymagne I was expecting him to produce. Ah well it might be tumblers but it was real bubbles! He asked me to open the bottle as he had never opened a bottle of champagne before. I thought I'd pass on my learnt technique, from an older man, of holding the cork still and gently coaxing the bottle round until you feel the cork coming out gradually, but felt like I was teaching him how to give birth: "Easy does it" "Turn it slowly" "Breath and relax" etc. It didn't bode well when the cork exploded out of the bottle and my face was sprayed with champagne.

We rescued the rest of the bubbles and enjoyed drinking it. Now this is where it gets naughty. Mike confessed he had always wanted to pour and drink champagne from a lady's garden so to speak. Well I was game if he was . Oh my god, I cannot even begin to describe what happened next, my poor lady bits were soaked and slurped like a child with a mr whippy ice cream! It wasn't funny it was tragic, I couldn't even direct him as I had the bed sheet in my mouth to stop me laughing/crying.

Mercifully he stopped and suggested we move on. Have you any condoms? I asked. No came the answer, luckily I was a well organised girl and had a stash. I gave him a condom and he fiddled around like i have never seen trying to put it on until in the end I asked if it was his first time? No he said but my other partners were on the pill and didn't mind me being bareback. I said "well sorry mate I do, so get it on." He then turned to face me and said as he'd pleasured me with the champagne I should pleasure him by putting the condom on and made gestures to indicate that I should do this not with my hands!! Well at this point I thought, ok,

I got away without returning the bubble favour but if this guy thinks putting a condom on is foreplay, I'm not liking my chances of a satisfying evening here. So, I backed out gracefully using the, I'm sorry but I'm too drunk to sh** you and don't want to regret it tomorrow line. He let me out of the smelly house calling me a c**k tease all the way down from the attic. Well come on ladies we have to put our foot down sometimes!

Yet another disastrous evening!!!

The Arabian Knight

Bored on a Sunday so thought I would sign onto t'internet and see what was going on! Inundated by emails and requests to chat I gradually worked my way down the chat list trying to remember who I had said what to, given the volume of guys wanting to chat and the fact that I still had a fuzzy head from the night before!! Too much vino….. again! When will I learn? NEVER!! Probably!! It was Saturday night after all and I had a couple of rather nice bottles of red in the wine rack! (did have anyway!)

I noticed one guy who was being extra persistent in his request to chat – his identity on the site was "witwam" or something like that!! He was 6'0.5" tall (the half inch was very important to him as he referred to it on a number of occasions over the course of 4 weeks or so when we first got chatting! Not sure why!) He (I will refer to him as T for the purposes of this book) told me he originated from Beirut and had lived in the UK for about 20 years and had studied at 2 Universities Manchester and Liverpool – great I thought, he has a brain!! He didn't have a picture up on his profile however said he would send one to me via my own email address if I would give it to him. Fine, I thought, he can't physically track me down if I shared it with him, so eagerly awaited a first glimpse of his apparently stunning looks!! Being Arabic he must be dark and handsome as he said he was of slim build and of course 6'0.5" tall!! (Sudden visions of a young Omar Sherif appeared riding a black Arab stallion through the desert wearing white!) He told me he was going through a divorce at the time, however wasn't a problem as he had purchased another house for him to live in and his future ex-wife was still in the marital home! The divorce was amicable and they were still in contact because of access to their 2 children.

A few days went by and still I hadn't receive a picture of him, however he kept promising to send one when he got the chance. He informed me that his wife was currently in Spain purchasing a house over there for herself and would be back in two weeks. In the meantime he was looking after the children and therefore was unable to meet with me any sooner. He asked me if I would like to meet him for dinner once his wife returned and he was free from his babysitting duties. Of course, I replied I would love to meet him. T duly googled a number of restaurants near to us and suggested a fish restaurant which was a little expensive, however the food was excellent!! We pencilled in arrangements of what time we were going to meet and where. He told me that he would wait for me on the car park as he would NEVER allow his lady to enter a restaurant on her own!! At last, I thought, a real gentleman!! I asked him what type of car he drove so I could keep my eye out for him on the car park...... reply "Very dark grey Mercedes E-class" – wow – classy I thought!!

I did remind him that it would be really good to see a picture of him before we met, and indeed he did eventually send one over to me. My heart did a bit of a flutter as I saw the email in my inbox with an attachment...... Oh gosh!! Here goes I said out loud..... "Wow" "He is absolutely stunning" I said to myself...... he was dark, very handsome, my perfect man!! I was bowled over and couldn't wait to meet him now

I had seen a picture of him. The days seemed very long and a week or so seemed ages ago.

I would very often open the email he had sent to me with his picture in just to get a 'fix' of his stunning looks, and on one particular day I noticed something rather strange….. as I moved my cursor around the screen, as you do to navigate, it had remained hovering over his picture for a few seconds and suddenly a weblink appeared at the end of the arrow….. "www/menskincare.com"….. What the hell's going on now I wondered…. I followed the link which took me to this skin care website and yes it did have lots of guys pictures on there advertising their products….. I scanned the pages to see if the same picture came up….. Nope nothing there that I could find! The next time we were chatting on IM I did ask him about the link to which he replied "I have no idea, I asked the computer shop to scan it in for me as I am not very tecky" He explained that the picture had been taken on the balcony of his beach hut back in Lebanon which is why he was looking downwards. He also explained that photographers often appeared on the beach taking family photos!!! I decided to park this one for a while.

I asked him if I could have his mobile number (as he had mine) so I could text him and we could keep in touch (at that time he was totally in control of the situation as I couldn't initiate any contact with him apart from email. He went on to explain that he didn't have a mobile phone. With him having his own business he had been continuously pestered by his employees, suppliers, customers etc and had lost his temper one day and thrown it out of the car window and to this day he refuses to have one!! Strange, I thought, how can he run a business with minimal contact? His business was property development in Beirut (forgot to mention that one!) He explained that he was in the process of developing

12 luxury villas which were to be built just on the outskirts of Beirut as the centre was all high-rise structures due to the way the mountain range surrounded the city making space scarce!

He talked to me about his 2 children and how he would like me to meet them at some stage, T said that he wanted me all ways always!!

He explained that he conducted his business whilst in the UK over the internet and home telephone line, which he didn't want to give me at the moment as he didn't know me and because of his kids at this early stage. Fine I thought, I will go with the flow. T said that he would fly out to Beirut every few months as he had an office there as well as a beach house!! Gosh, this only gets better, I thought as he asked me if I would like to join him on one of his trips!!

T also told me that he had a Stud Farm and bred Arabs in the Lebanon and one day he would love me to visit the farm with him!!!

T did ring me one day from a mobile phone whilst he was allegedly at the bank – he had borrowed his eldest sons phone to call me, however had withheld the number......
OK I can understand the reason for that too, I will give him the benefit of the doubt even though I got this strange feeling that his voice did not match the picture he had sent to me! His voice sort of conjured up this vision of an overweight Arabian guy who was a heavy smoker as it sounded as though he was having difficulty breathing!! I may be wrong but that was at the back of my mind!!

The weekend was eventually approaching and I couldn't wait to see him, and he me!! His wife was due back in the country the evening before. Fantastic, everything was on track and I started to think about what I should wear to make a good first impression!! Has to be the little black classy number with new heels and black stockings……… This guy could be my future!!

The day before we were planning to meet I received an email from him sent at 01.43am saying…….

"am so so sorry was not able to contact you, (even though he did have my mobile number!) i received a phone call from home and extremely bad news , have no alternative but to fly back immediately

been busy to sort out many a thing

am so sorry and apologise

pray god you understand

T ….. "

So, Surprise, Surprise,(NOT!) the dinner date never happened!!!

Understand what? I asked myself!! Do I look as though I have a bloody crystal ball??!!!! Here we go again I said to myself, yet another PLONKER! But no, give him the benefit of the doubt as this guy may JUST be genuine!! So I emailed him back and asked what was wrong, I hoped everything gets sorted (whatever everything was!) and let me know when he is likely to be back.

Strange coincidence that this also happened on the same day his future ex-wife was due back so he would be child free!!! I did start to check out flight times and dates from Manchester to Beirut, but that wouldn't tell me anything anyway!!!

Mmmmm, the jury is still out on this one!! Was he telling the truth or not! What do you think ladies??..............

A few days later I received an email from him as follows…. "good morning

my brother with his sun were involved in a serious car accident - both are still in intensive care, unfortunately my nephew is still in a very critical situation,

at moment sorry as i am unable to give a definite date for my return.

hope your days are good ones

T…. xx"

I obviously replied and said that I hoped everything works out OK and that his nephew recovers, to which I receive this reply "good morning

hope so and doctors are confident he will recover, believe it or not, yes am @ office doing some work. Are you in shock hahaha are u at office ??? just opened my msn but you are not to be seen, left you a message there

are u so busy at work????

T…..xx

So suspicious sally here decides to check out his IP address from the recent emails he had sent and guess what!!???? They were from a location in MANCHESTER and NOT Beirut!!

Yes you guessed it! Yet another Asshole!! What is that all about then?

Jim Lad!!

I did however meet someone last night for a drink - he looked fine on his profile and was looking for a long term relationship! That will do I thought, let's meet up with him and see if there are any sparks there! We met on a public car park, I drove up to his car to find that it was empty!! Strange I thought, he had text me to tell me he had arrived and that he was waiting for me on the car park. As I glanced to my right, I spot this guy who looked similar to the one on the website, but a lot slimmer! "He's obviously lost some weight " I thought to myself as he walked towards me. Mmmm, I thought he looks a lot older than he does on his profile! As our eyes made contact I smiled, and of course he smiled back to me too!! "Jeez" I was suddenly plunged into a scene from the Pirates of the Carribean film with Johny Depp....... He had NO white teeth!!! Oh my!! he reminded me of a scene from Tom and Jerry the cartoon when Tom had had his tail plugged into an electrical socket by Jerry the mouse, and electrocuted!! Remember when all his extremeties turned black and frazzled? Well that's what his teeth were like!! BLACK and frazzled - YUK! it was awful!! He must have lived on fags and he had obviously not shown his teeth on his profile picture and something that I didn't ask him about! ie what colour were his teeth? lmao!! Oh my, what do I do? Do I turn and run or go for a quick drink with him? Me being me, I decided to go for a drink with him, try not to look at his teeth for the next half hour or so and then run!! I suppose if HE is the one, then he could always go to the dentist – remember, I said to myself, it is the person that counts not his teeth!!   As we walked to the pub he held my hand, told me that I was gorgeous and immediately said he would like to see me again…. I was praying that I wouldn't see anyone I knew over the next half hour!!! We chatted for a short time and he could see that I wasn't bowled over by him, so I said let's just leave it for now and we could just be friends. We parted ways.

He text me the next morning after I had indicated that that he wasn't the one for me and we had different life styles, and accused me of being a player!! The cheeky TWAT perhaps I should have told him about his personal hygiene and dog breath, but I just didn't have the heart to tell him to sort his BLOODY AWFUL BLACK TEETH OUT!!! God, can you imagine what the state of his socks and underpants would be like? I just dread to think!! So, tip for the future, put on your profile that Black Teeth are a Turn Off and Personal Hygiene is a Turn On!! Pity you can't have access to a 'Smelly Cam" to check them out before you meet with them!!!

Lessons learnt, lessons learnt!!

Profile Names
(a bit of a different theme for a while!)

I really don't understand why guys use rather strange profile names on these sites!!! The vision that some of these names conjure up are really a BIG TURN OFF!! guys.... So think seriously about what you call yourself? Perhaps you could ask your wife for those who are married! Lol!!

"Reindeer" does this guy have a red nose and have a little 'tail'? Or does he only come out at Christmas time? Or is his real name really Rudolf and wants to just lead you into this truth gently?

"Lostboy666"...... thinks he is a little devil but rather confused.com? Or is he in search of a motherly girlfriend? MILF springs to mind!!

"Scotty107dog"........ grey hair? Fluffy personality? Short legs? Dribbles with tongue hanging out?.......... or does he have a fetish for wearing tartan dog collars with matching lead and hold-ups with nothing else?......

"Devonbull"....... Well, what can I say to this one? Are there a lot of bulls in Devon or is there a lot of bulls**t in Devon? Or does he think he is as well hung as a bull? What a load of b****cks!!

"Littleoldme"...... what sort of a picture does this conjure up?....... someone who is frail and feels sorry for themselves with not much outlook on life!!!! Certainly doesn't capture my attention…….. ☹

"Twoodle"…….. reminded me of a cheap pot noodle – you look forward to indulging in a hot steamy session only to wish you hadn't indulged afterwards as you're still hungry and feel crap…… think I will give this one a miss too!!

Internet confessions ...

Paul was easy company and had a gentle humour. I already knew from his profile that he was divorced with a daughter who lived with her mother but spent weekends with him. He seemed a nice, regular guy during the email and phone conversations. Conversation flowed throughout dinner. Then coffee arrived. He started by saying he had something to tell me that he felt had not been appropriate to email or mention over the phone, but that I should know about before the decision to meet again, or not. "Thing is ... I'm on probation for physically assaulting my ex-wife. Oh dear, I can tell by your face that you're not comfortable with this ..." We didn't meet again.

In their own words.....
The long and somewhat depressing!!......

"Hello and welcome , thank you for viewing , the show will commence as soon as you click the send button !!so, can you please turn off all mobiles before we begin !! ok, my hobbies are Northern soul , has been my passion for many a moon , Vintage scooter restoration on my 2nd this year,, as in vespas and lambrettas , photography , and i play the odd game called golf . and yes i play it oddly !! i enjoy cooking ,for 2 is better than for 1 ,and can do legendary irish coffees ! but hopeless at dish washing ,great at plate smashing though , love the outdoors , especially camping in the summer , i will camp in any hotel ! enjoy spontaneous days out , but not combustiable ! Winters on its way out or is it back ? that big yellow ball is re appearing , whats the maddest , wackiest or zaniest thing the sun did to you ? all answers on the back of a postcard please. To coincide with our summer , quickly turning to autumn ! I have a real log fire , plenty of wine and dvds , to fill a cliche !!!! but what is missing ????.and its not the wood ! Whats your longest relationship , how boring , my question to you the public is.... Whats your shortest relationship ? please put your answer in the subject box and i will reply with mine .....i bet i win ! I have old fashioned views and believe romance is not dead ....it may need reviving though I look for and like femininty in a lady ie heels , perfume etc ,(oh and heels) maybe you could say how feminine you are and why !!!! Wearing my heart on my sleeve , literally not latteraly , i am an open book with many un full filled chapters , this will be ammeneded throughout the year prize for the maddest message !! , try it you may like it ! thats what me old mum said to me when i was growing up , never did make brocoli taste better !if you agree,email, if you disagree email! PS , the rooney is a name given to me by an old friend , im not irish as once asked !. according to this site , i am now 60% completed !!! i was looking for 100 % ah well better than my school reports !anyway who ever gets 100% ? If your a soulie , get in touch , if you have to ask whats a soulie , dont bother asking Who remembers this???....Close your eyes and go back in time... Before the Internet... Before semi-automatics, joyriders and crack.... Before SEGA or Super Nintendo... Way back..... I'm talking about Hide and Seek in the park. The corner shop. Butterscotch. Football with an old can. Fingerbob. Beano, Dandy, Buster, and Dennis the Menace. Roly Poly, jumping the stream, building dams. The smell of the sun and fresh cut grass. Bazooka Joe bubble gum. An ice cream cone on a warm summer night from the van that plays a tune. vanilla or strawberry or perhaps a screwball. Wait...... The Corona pop man with all differnt colours or were they flavours in funny shaped bottles ! Watching Saturday morning cartoons, short commercials or the flicks. Children's Film Foundation, The Double Deckers, Red Hand Gang, Tiswas or Swapshop?, and 'Why Don't You'? When around the corner seemed far away and going into town seemed like going somewhere. Earwigs, wasps, stinging nettles and bee stings and frogs pawn that looked like semolina !!! Collecting catapillers puttung them in a box with lots of grass, thinking of them as your pets, and next morning they all dried up and totally dead as a wot not, and you cant undersatand why, perhaps they needed some air holes!!Sticky fingers. Playing Marbles. Ball bearings. Big 'uns and Little 'uns. Cops and Robbers, Cowboys and Indians, and Zorro. Rag and bone man shouting any ol irrrrron and the Sunday morning paper boy wearing clip cloppy noisy shoes to wake everyone up on purpose !!! Climbing trees. Making igloos out of snow banks. Walking to school, no matter what the weather. Running till you were out of breath, laughing so hard that your stomach hurt, Jumping on the bed. Pillow fights. Spinning around on roundabouts, getting dizzy and falling down was cause for giggles. Being tired from playing.... remember that? The worst embarrassment was being picked last for a team. Water balloons were the ultimate weapon. Football cards in the spokes transformed any bike into a motorcycle. Choppers and Grifters and wait for this one ...Space hoppers !and what about Clackers to bruise your arms !!. Eating raw jelly. Orange squash ice pops. Vimto and Jubbly lollies Remember when... There were two types of trainers - girls and boys, and Dunlop Green Flash The only time you wore them at School was for P.E. And they were called gym shoes or if you are older - plimsoles You knew everyone in your street - and so did your parents. It wasn't odd to have two or three 'best' friends. You didn't sleep a wink on Christmas Eve. When nobody owned a pure-bred dog. When 25p was decent pocket money , Gluing 2p pieces to the floor outside your house and laffing ya dirty socks off when someone tried to pick up inconspiciuosly !Curly Whirlys. Space Dust. Toffo's. Top Trumps and Spangles , what ever were the tan coloured ones ??? When you'd reach into a muddy gutter for a penny. When nearly everyone's mum was at home when the kids got there. When any parent could discipline any kid, or feed him or use him to carry groceries and nobody, not even the kid, thought a thing of it. When being sent to the head's office was nothing compared to the fate that awaited a misbehaving pupil at home. Basically, we were in fear for our lives but it wasn't because of drive-by shootings, drugs, gangs etc. Parents and grandparents were a much bigger threat and some of us are still afraid of them. Didn't that feel good? Just to go back and say, Yeah, I remember that! Remember when.... Decisions were made by going 'Ip, Dip, Dog Sht' 'Race issue' meant arguing about who ran the fastest. Money issues were handled by whoever was the banker in Monopoly The worst thing you could catch from the opposite sex was germs. And the worst thing in your day was having to sit next to one. It was unbelievable that 'British Bulldog 123' wasn't an Olympic event. Having a weapon in school, meant being caught with a catapult. Nobody was prettier than Mum. Scrapes and bruises were kissed and made better. Taking drugs meant orange-flavoured chewable aspirin. Ice cream was considered a basic food group. Getting a foot of snow was a dream come true. Older siblings were the worst tormentors, but also the fiercest protectors. If you can remember most or all of these, then you have LIVED. Rhubarb and custards , Sherbet Dips, Texan Bars , Sugar Butties, spit washes! (oh man! Lol), Harvest Festival (was a good time for your parents to clear out all the riff raff from the cupboards!), Spanish tobacco (coconut flavoured candy!) 'Can you imagine trying to push that to kids now-a-days, what with the nanny state an' all.......''

Jeez, I thought, would I ever get a word in edge ways with this guy? Is he stuck in the past? Mmmmmm, maybe I will give this one a miss.....

Example 2

"Well i am a grumpy Victor Meldrew complaining old git with sexual libido of a dead squid

Let me say unlike Victor i aint loaded far from it but what i have to give well you cant buy but i have loads of it to give for free to the right person

I also want to say that i can be the most thickest sdaftest we didnt person you may know and yeh may have a sulk and a rant but dont we all god if we'd be bonkers by now but if we do hit it off you can't ask for a more loyal trusting loving partner who will love you.... sorryif it sounds soft

well there it goes the only lie i'm goona tell you AND BY THE WAY I HATE PEOPLE WHO DO LIE there is just no need cos you get found out in the end. And for all those who are vain....beauty doesn't give you a right to lie. LECTURE OVER HAHA.

If you message me i will respond as i fell it is only polite. Unfortunately because of this it means i get blocked if i try messaging people cos of their restrictions. If i look at your profile if you look at mine and are interested please message me as i may not be able to contact you. also the chances are that if i have looked at your profile and not messaged you then i most probably think you are out of my league and wouldn't respond anyway so feel free to message me and it would make my day (god i sound so insecure, but better to be honest)not that those who i do message aren't if you know what i mean (best stop digging this hole as getting deeper in it haha)

Yes i do own my own home which means that i have a mortgage and bills to pay but i do have some spare cash a month but loads. so anybody looking for some kind of walking bank had better keep walking themselves haha though saying that i aint a skinflint and will give whatever i can to the right person.

Do you know those guys who always no matter what clothes they throw on look smart and distinguished well all i can say is i aint one of them ha ha

so I'm not really sure what to say here as been disappointed in the past just wanting I suppose like most of us on here to try and find that right person. Still actively play sport and reasonably fit but could do better, have realised a long time ago the days of the 6 pack have gone ha ha.

I like most types of music but don't like Jazz, Reggae and especially dislike Boy/Girl bands who just cover other peoples music all time.

Have been sepearated for altogether 3 years. i have a dog who I love to pieces. If you are interested drop me a line and I will get back to you.

I think it is only fair for me to point out now that unfortunately i don't drive. I think by telling you now it saves for disappointment later as it has done in the past"

Question then is.... What on earth would I be interested in? I would probably get in touch with this guy if I wanted to slit my wrists in the very near future!!! NOT!!! Oh dear..... it's a shame!!!

I won't put any more of these in this book as it may just drive you to despair too soon!! So here are some shorter profiles that I thought may amuse you!!!

The short......

"Rusty older guy. BUT honest. Say Hi and I will return the compliment" – his fave sport was Ice-hockey – come on girls...... would your REALLY be interested in this guy?

"take me as I am...dont like to have a pacific chat up line. Every encounter is different" – well, he either has a warped sense of humour or genuinely can't spell!! Either way, I think I will stick with the Atlantic!!!

"they call me shrek and im looking for my princess !!"....... Mmmmm, think I will give this one a miss..... I wonder how often he changes his underpants and socks??!!! YUK!!

"I'm looking for someone who has kids, preferably, but if not that's o.k. Someone who loves life no matter what it throws at them. Someone outgoing, spontaneous, romantic, who loves the outdoors. I want someone compatible with me and what I like. You must have a good personality and my daughter must like you right away. She is all I live for so if she doesn't like you then I won't, no offense but kids are the best judge in character"...... Oh my, doesn't sound as though you would have much of a say in this relationship.... Whoever it is with.. The father or the daughter?!!!!!??? DO NOT TOUCH WITH A BARGE POLE!!!!

"Are you lonesome tonight? tired of suspicious minds..Want to Love Me Tender and Be My Teddy Bear? Then I Can't Help Falling in Love with you and i need your love tonight.

But, please stay away if you've lost that loving feeling or you're All Shook Up also if you have a wooden heart, and are Devil in Disguise, so if you want to Step On My Blue Suede Shoes, or frequent the Heartbreak Hotel, you Hound Dog... don't be cruel, i'm looking for some-one with a burning love to be the girl of mine, some-one i just can't help believing in, if that's you then lets live the impossible dream, drop me a line i promise it'll not be returned to sender"...... Bit of an Elvis fan then do you think? I bet he's got a specially made white Elvis cat suit covered in bling with a big collar waiting to surprise you one night!!!....... I think I left the building before I entered it....... MOVE ON!!!

"Ding Dong"........ Yes, this ryhms with King Kong!!!! Plonker!!! NEXT!!!

The Strange…..or amusing!!!

"I could be a paper…you can scribe your anger,use me to absorb tears..don't throw me after use..'coz u are feeling cold i will burn myself to keep u warm…i make adjustments flexible to whoever i may facing,in that way i can easily gain friends…i love to help people up of their problems but i keep problems to myself,i only express myself and emotions to anyone who suits taste with….i value friendship that will go out of my way to nurture one,i wouldn't say i am ordinary,i am unique in every way…i love talking to people,exchange thoughts and dreams…intellectual intercourse,i've been always a survivor..strong-willed at all times,but at the same time i am trying to iron-up past mistakes and pick up some pieces of my life which myself scattered….i am looking for the day that my mind is totally free,i believe that all people are good that's why i always get in trouble in trusting easily….i am hoping that one day i could finally have some one face to face with all my life..only a matter of time that i could build my happy family…" What on earth is this all about? Sounds like a bit of a disaster zone to me….. Avoid at all costs!!!! NEXT!

"especially from cupcake. Really special type of cake. sweet a bit complex and fruity but a compelling and mindblowing mixture. Really tasty and soft in the middle. Fantastic !!!!!!!!!!!!!" ……. I wonder what he would wear on a first date? Multi-coloured jumper with a sprinkling of icing sugar/dandruff on his eyebrows?.......... I won't be finding out first hand that's for sure......... NEXT!!!

"I am a dynamic figure, often seen scaling walls and crushing ice, I have been known to remodel shopping centres on my lunch breaks, making them more efficient in the area of heat retention. I translate ethnic slurs for Cuban refugees, I write award-winning operas, I manage time efficiently. Occasionally, I tread water for three days in a row. I woo women with my sensuous and god like saxaphone playing. I can pilot bicycles up severe inclines with unflagging speed. I cook Thirty-Minute meals in less than twenty minutes. I am an expert in poultry management, a veteran in love, and an outlaw in Peru. Using only a hoe and a large glass of water, I once single-handedly defended a small village in the Amazon Basin from a horde of ferocious army ants. When I'm bored, I build large suspension bridges in my garden. On Wednesdays, after work, I repair electrical appliances free of charge. I am an abstract artist, a concrete analyst, and a ruthless bookie.Critics worldwide swoon over my original line of corduroy evening wear. I don't perspire. I am a private citizen, yet I receive fan mail. Children trust me. I can hurl tennis rackets at small moving objects with deadly accuracy. I once read Paradise Lost, Moby**** and David Copperfield in one day and still had time to refurbish an entire dining room that evening. I know the exact location of every food item in the supermarket. I have performed several covert operations for the government. I sleep once a week; when I do sleep, I sleep in a chair. While on vacation in Denmark, I successfully negotiated with a group of terrorists who had seized a small bakery. The laws of physics do not apply to me. I balance, I weave, I dodge, I frolic, and my bills are all paid. On weekends, to let off steam, I participate in full-contact origami. Years ago I discovered the meaning of life but forgot to write it down. I have made extraordinary four course meals using only a toaster. I breed prizewinning clams. I have won bullfights in Spain, cliff-diving awards in Sri Lanka, and chess competitions at the Kremlin. I have played wih Nicole Kidmans body., I have performed open-heart surgery, and I have spoken with elvis." What a nutcase!!! Steer Clear of this one......... NEXT!!!

.

Internet male dating opening gambits ... (ie emails received by way of first contact)

"Hi there x ... I'm intelligent, good looking, confident and the sort of bloke you would like to have run off with but I never asked you to.".......... What on earth is THAT all about? I can't even muster up the energy to make sense of this one!! Over to you guys.... What's the rationale behind this one?

"Good afternoon gorjus! ... Due to my night time job (which, surprisingly is not as a full time philanderer or snake charmer!.......... Obviously in a relationship if he can only meet in the daytime!), I can only meet daytimes so you'll need to be free for coffee, lunch and, where the chemistry is right - long desserts. I might even dispense with lunch for the right woman but I'm afraid the coffee is non-negotiable." On his profile he said he was 6' 7", on his picture he wore a headscarf on his head (you know the type the WWF guys wear when not in the ring! Hulk Hogan type I was thinking of!) which was a US flag accessorised by a skinny looking snake hanging around his neck!!!! (yes it was his pet snake) Given the fact that a) I work in the day, b) I am on a no carbohydrate diet and despise Hulk Hogan and things dangling from different body parts, I never made the effort to meet this guy – Hellraiser something or other I think his profile name was!

"… I'm the type of guy your mother would have warned you about from marrying, saying I wasn't the faithful type. She was right. What would my mother have warned me about you?" TWAT!!!…….. No further comments from me on this occasion!!

"… If the only photo you can show me is in sepia, or from how you looked some years ago when you were considerably more attractive than now, then please don't bother. Whilst we're on the subject, I also don't want to see any wedding photos, school photos, photos with babies, dogs or loose bits dangling about."…. What do you want then? Gosh, he sounds like a bundle of laughs!!! NOT!!

"… I'm looking for advice about suitable attire as fashion remains a mystery to me – can you help?" answer…. NO!!!………

"…You are a paragon to behold. Only Gods creation can compare to the beauty i see in you…your beauty got me speechless pretty..Can i get to know more about you?"… Oh my, who is this? Shakespeare resurrected?….. PASS!!!!

"… You're attractive, confident but need some attention. You look like a woman, act like a woman and know how to treat a man, and I'd like to apply for that position (please)."…. Well, strangely enough, I AM a woman who knows how to treat a man….. However not currently advertising for any fruitcake!!!…… NEXT!!!

"… If you find a spider in your hair or in the room I will deal with it in a nice way, as long as it not a lethal one in which case I shall kill it with my strong legs (it would have been removed from your hair first).".…… WHAT? Is THAT all about?… lost for words yet again!!……

"… I'm looking for Passion with a big "P" (if you've mis-read that and think I'm looking with my big P for Passion, apologies). Don't reply if you only want passion with a small "p" because I'm not your man. If you're looking for passion with any other combination of upper and lower case, there may be basis for negotiation. If you're looking for love, whether lower/upper case, script, italics, bold or underlined - then it's a big fat NO from me. Good. I think I've cleared that up".….. how boring would life be with this guy? NEXT!!!!

"… You look to be the thinking man's woman. I'm the thinking woman's man. Perhaps we can have some thoughts together? "…… I really don't think so.…. Too much thinking going on here for my liking.…!!! I prefer some action too!!

"… Did you know there is only one poisonous snake in England? It is an adder called Nigel. He lives in a field in Devon and is very dozy. He will only bite you if you poke him. If you want to be completely snake free go to Ireland (snakes do not like the rain).".…. 3 words to describe this one I think.….. LOST THE PLOT!!!……

"… When I walk into a room, men lower their heads and women throw their knickers at me. As a result, I tend to avoid crowds and have developed a mild form of agoraphobia so I rarely go out without my wife. I will endeavour to make an exception if we meet, but if it's not possible, I promise to leave her in the car with the engine running."…… sorry this just does NOT appeal to me.… Moving swiftly on!!!

"… I travel all over the UK (no, I'm not a train driver) and therefore, wherever you are, I will visit. No call-out charge."….. OK, I'm in outer Mongolia, will send you my address!!!!……

". . . I will make you laugh, groan, moan (subject to terms and conditions) and once met you'll see my soft under-belly and realise I'm just a regular, handsome Joe looking to hold and cherish someone."…. sorry Darlin but it was the 'soft under-belly' that REALLY didn't do it for me!!! Ooops!!

". . . I love kissing. Sharing long, passionate kisses is my favourite hobby. Unfortunately, my wife's favourite hobby is stamp-collecting and long passionate kissing makes it difficult to lick the little hinges afterwards, so we don't."….. Keep on collecting then…….. Jeez…. There are some loonies on these sites!!!!

"… What do I want? Normal! (with a capital "N"). Don't reply if you're size zero. If I can wrap my arms around you and still tickle my sides, or pick my belly button, you're too skinny. I might snap you. If you can't buy your clothes from a High Street store without having to visit the "strange shape" department then it's likely you'll attract too much attention on our date, and that just won't do. If you've got flat feet, can't wear heels, have some medical condition, bits missing (or heaven forbid - bits added), a history of mental instability or delusions of grandeur, then you have my sympathy but not my adoration. Similarly, if your mother tongue is not english, but a strange dialect of "txt" talk and you're incapable of messaging me without slipping an "lol" in or finishing off with a row of "x"'s, then we will find it difficult to communicate. Finally, if you think you look cool in trainers, track suits or combat trousers then you're either horrific, or worse, a man. If you wear double-gusset knickers instead of skimpy sexy panties because they're more comfortable then I'm afraid they're destined to remain unexplored. So, by a process of elimination, that probably only leaves YOU. If you don't like the sound of me, then please ignore everything I've written. I'll conform. Blimey, I'm so easy"... OMG, I wonder what HE is really like? It does make you wonder what their mental condition is when you read things like this...... he never received a reply by the way!!!......

"hi am ian and hi am a x h.g.v drive and hi av a steel pin in my left arm but it is ok now"...... I am soooo glad that his left arm is OK now..... Gosh what an exciting night out you would have with this guy..... Can you imagine going on holiday with him and listening to the same story each time you went through the body scanner!!! I think I will give his left arm a miss on this occasion......It gets worse not better!!!

Eye Eye!!!
(Back to a few more real life encounters....)

Andy had made first contact with me via a message asking me how the dating was going on the site, to which I replied "It isn't!". We got chatting via email for a few weeks, he seemed to be a down to earth person, not someone who would set the world alight, but someone who may be Mr Reliable.... for a change!! He was very slim, similar height as me, maybe an inch taller, receding hair line so kept what he had left very short (not quite shaved). He had been married once, (and still was on paper) and had been separated for about 2 years. He had his own house and worked as an HGV Driver.

On one particular Saturday we had been emailing each other for a couple of hours, when Andy asked me if I was doing anything the following day? Well, I didn't have any particular plans so told him no, I was free. He asked me if I would be interested in meeting with him for a drink? Fine, I replied and duly made arrangements to meet at a local pub on Sunday afternoon. He told me what car he drove (a little tiny matchbox one!) so I could find him on the car park (how many times do I have to do this? It's getting monotonous!!)

We met the next day as agreed and went into the pub to buy a drink – of course I offered to pay, however he was happy to buy me a J2O – orange and passion fruit flavour!!

(a glass of chilled white wine on the patio would be better!!)
The weather was a bit mixed, sun and cloud and rain so
had to keep moving around the table to be either under the
umbrella when it rained and then not under the umbrella
when the sun came out – it quickly became a game of musical
chairs!!! Oh well, remain chilled I thought to myself!! After
about half an hour, as he ran across the car park to get his
sunglasses out of his car, it suddenly dawned on me that I
had learned sooooo much about mountain bikes and race
bikes!! Andy informed me that he had a collection of 6 bikes
which were worth about £2K each on average! Oh my, he
was rather keen, I suddenly felt VERY unfit!! He told me
that he would cycle at least 30 miles each day – mmmm,
I thought, maybe this guy could be good for me, a breath
of fresh air and influence my 'keep fit' regime!! (wouldn't
be hard as I didn't really do that much exercise – the odd
walk here and there and that was about it!!) He returned
back to his seat from across the other side of the car park
(large one) like a jack rabbit!! Bloody hell, that was quick!!
He doesn't mess about does he! (I wonder if he's the same
in the bedroom I thought!) After a few hours he explained
to me that he doesn't normally do this, but wondered if I
would like to come back to his for a coffee – he said he felt
comfortable and trusted me!! And to be honest, I felt rather
the same way, so that was OK – I knew the area which was a
built up area so if I did scream then I'm sure someone would
hear me!! So off we set, me following him in our cars. We
arrived about 5 minutes later and parked at the front of the
house while he parked in the drive (shared drive with the
neighbours he didn't really speak to - a bit of trivia but an
important feature!!).

We went into the kitchen to make a cup of tea and Andy had
a beer. He showed my around his garden which was well

kept along with a greenhouse in the corner which was full of tomatoes and peppers!! Very domesticated I thought as he rattled off the different dishes he likes to cook. Mmmm, maybe I will get an invite to dinner one day….. We will see!!

We then ventured into the garage where I was greeted by what looked like a huge pile of steel frames and wheels!! Wow!! This guy WAS serious about his bikes. Sat amongst this pile of steel and wheels and mud was the most stunning Suzuki bike - it looked like something off Nightrider, black, sleek, sexy, powerful with lots of WOW factor….. Gosh, I hope he takes me out on that one day, that would be fantastic!!

Anyway we return to the living room just chatting about anything and listening to his music collection which was unusual and huge!! I finished my tea and made a move at which point he asked when we could meet again. Ooooh! that's good I thought, I know there wasn't any chemistry there for me at that point but wondered if this would appear eventually if we got to know each other better. I agreed to meet with him again, he seemed quite harmless, and we arranged to meet the following weekend and go for a walk. Andy couldn't meet in the week because of his job ie up early and travelling around the country, so the weekend was the first opportunity we had.

The Saturday came around and during the week we had exchanged a few text messages just to say how are you and "howz ur day going?" type messages so nothing earth shattering!! I picked him up from his house at 11.00am and drove to a well known part of the countryside that has lots of walks and a great pub that does lovely pub food!!! Off we went and walked for a couple of hours, sat and chatted about life in general, but the main focus of the conversation was about where he worked - talk about gloom and doom!!! I nearly slit my wrists after an hour!!! - during all of this time there was no physical contact at all - not even a peck on the cheek when he got into my car, the only thing he was worried about was what clothes he was going to need and did he have the right ones in his carrier bag?

After our walk I suggested going to the pub for a bite to eat to which he replied, "Happy to go for a drink but I don't eat in the day"....... OK, I thought, we will just go for a drink and then I will go home and make some lunch for myself!! (What a miserable git - or was he just tight with money?) When we were at the bar I offered to pay for the drinks but he politely turned me down and said he would get them.... Well that's fair enough as I had paid for the petrol to get to where we were (and it wasn't just around the corner either!) I did start to feel rather embarrassed as he rummaged around in his purse for what seemed to be 5 minutes trying to find the right change... (yes, I did say purse! You know those sort of horse shoe shaped flat leather look things that have a flap on them!!!) Eventually he paid for the drinks and we went outside to the court yard to sit in the sun before we headed back home..... Talk about a 'cardboard cut-out', it would have been more exciting to be out with a 'cardboard cut-out' - I decided that his personality had done a runner or maybe it was cowering in the corner of his greenhouse with his tomatoes!!! Mmmm, I thought, this is NOT going to work is it? No matter how many times I see this guy it is NOT going to get any better!! Or should I give him another chance? Maybe I should, maybe I'm being a bit too critical too soon!!

As I dropped him off at the end of his drive we arranged to do the same the following week but go to a different place and try a different walk. We agreed on the final detail and said bye - I did give him a peck on his cheek before he got out of the car!!! Still no sparks though!

During that week Andy sent me a text telling me he couldn't make the weekend as we had planned as he had already made arrangements to go mountain biking with his friend, and had forgotten about it! OK, no worries I replied, we can re-arrange and asked him to let me know when he was free. A couple of weeks later on the Saturday evening I was at a family gathering when I received a text from him…. I could tell that it was a picture message from the icon on my phone…. Oh! This is a turn up for the book I thought and clicked on the message… a few seconds later I was greeted by this picture that looked like something out of a horror movie!!! It was a close up of his eye!! A very RED eye!!! "Was there any need for him to send me THAT?" YUK!! I replied and asked how he had done it and he replied and said he just woke up with it like that!! I advised him to go to A and E to get it checked out…… over the next week or so I received the odd joke text from him which I didn't find funny at all so didn't bother replying……. He was too exciting for me….. (NOT!) I would certainly end up in a early grave or getting very old and boring very quickly!!! NOT for me I'm afraid! I don't do getting old very gracefully or at all!! Im in denial and will be forever young!! Who indeed says you have to get old and conform to expectations like wearing flat shoes and tan tights and pushing one of those square shopping trollies on wheels…….. NO CHANCE!!! EVER!! ….. Needless to say I never saw or heard from him again…. I'm sure he is very happy surrounded by his tomatoes and basil filled home, but it would have been rather fun to go out on his motorbike!!!

NEXT!!!

Black from the Black Country

Maybe I should try dating a black guy next time…. I had had plenty of messages and requests to meet black guys….. Why not I thought, the next black guy who contacts me and I like the look and sound of I will arrange to meet!!! Kerching!! Within a couple of weeks this black guy, Jo, who had been trying to chat to me for some time sent me another message and asked how I was and how the dating was going. I replied basically saying it wasn't!! He described himself as 6'1", large framed, single, never been married, no children, had his own house, a non-smoker, just bought a new car (Audi A5 sport - very nice!) self-employed doing electrical work, TV's, stereos, alarms and that type of work. He also had a dog called Bruff, a Staffordshire bull terrier who was soft as anything and loved Pringles!!

He explained that most of his clients were local however did have some clients near to where I lived and when he was next in my area he would let me know and we could meet up for a drink. He also had a degree so had a brain!!! Fantastic…. He certainly ticks all of my boxes as far as I can see so far!! A few weeks went by and we chatted most days either via IM or phone as I had given him my mobile number so it would be easier to make arrangements to meet up.

Eventually we arranged to meet one Tuesday evening early after work - he made a special journey and drove down from Birmingham as he didn't have any client meetings any time soon and really was keen on us meeting sooner rather than later. All positive signs I thought, so I arranged to leave work earlier than normal which would give me time to get changed, put my make-up on and do my hair. We met on the car park of a Little Chef just off the motorway, his car was very impressive, white with those twinkly lights dotted around the headlights - classy!!! I looked into the drivers area to get a better look at him.... Gosh, he wasn't joking when he said that an Audi TT wasn't the model of his new car as he wouldn't be able to get into it!! He was HUGE!! And all muscle!!! Phew!!! I wonder if it's true what they say about black guys..... Well Hung?!! Who knows if we do get on and the chemistry is there I may find out......... Here's hoping!!! Jo didn't have a midlands accent even though he lived there, he originated from south of Watford so had a gentle, sexy southern accent.... NICE! ☺ He turned his car around to follow me to the nearest pub. When we got out of our cars he came over to me gave me a wonderful warm hug and a kiss on my lips - nothing cheesy or 'fish like', just a nice gently soft kiss!!! Wow, this man sure knows what to do with his lady.... I could just tell!!

We found our way into the pub, ordered drinks and sat on a lovely squashy sofa. The pub was an older pub which had been done up, it was on different levels to give it some character which was nice. Jo decided to order a bite to eat, I declined as I didn't really fancy anything on the menu as well as being rather nervous!! We started to chat and talk about about our life's journey's as you do, when all of a sudden this man on a microphone welcomed everyone to the Tuesday night quiz!!! Every time the quiz master spoke it was so loud that we had to halt the conversation until he finished asking the question...... needless to say, the conversation was something like a scene starring Normal Collier, you know, the comedian who used to pretend to wind his window up and down, sometimes you could hear him and then you couldn't!! It was rather funny and eventually we started to answer the quiz questions with everyone else!!

Jo ate his bacon and sausage baguette, which he said was awful, had another drink before scooting off back up to Birmingham. We had another cuddle and kiss (a bit longer this time!) and arranged to meet the following week. Great! This is looking good!!

The following week we met in a wine bar early one evening when he was on his way home from a client who lived not far from me which was rather handy!! We found a nice little corner in this trendy wine bar and Jo again ordered some food and some drinks - it was a really nice cuddly encounter, he was attentive and gave me the odd kiss on my cheek now and again. He felt very loving and he was keen to carry on seeing me, we even discussed me going over to his for the weekend in a few weeks and we could have a night out on the town - Broad Street I think he said which is where all the bars are and clubs!! Fantastic - deffo my type of guy!!

We couldn't make arrangements any earlier for a weekend together as Jo had been invited to a clients house warming party the weekend coming up and he was sorting out the music etc for it...... Not a problem! All over that weekend I never received any responses from any of my text messages - he did tell me that he kept his phone on silent and would only look at it when he was in the mood for chatting. I thought that perhaps he was hungover and didn't want being disturbed!! After about 4 days he text me to say that he wouldn't be able to make the following weekend as he had a problem with one of his eyes - one of his nephews had poked him in the eye when they had been play fighting and now it was infected!!! Great! I thought, you couldn't dream that one up could you!!! My suspicions were eliminated when I received a picture of his very swollen eye on my phone.... Not unless this is a 'blue peter' picture - one he had taken earlier and kept it on his phone!!! Stop being so suspicious I told myself.... This guy could be genuine and above all honest!! How refreshing would that be?

Over the next couple of weeks I got the odd text, no phone calls unless I called him and even then he didn't always answer or respond to any messages I may have left him. Then one day Jo text me to say he was in bed taking pain killers as his eye was still bad. He had been to A and E to get it lanced but they had advised him to just keep taking antibiotics and it would go down on it's own. I called him twice that day to see how he was but again no answer... how strange... perhaps he did meet or take someone to the party and has now had a change of heart in terms of meeting me again!! If this was the case, why could he just not say? Jo had mentioned the first night that we met that he did like his own space, maybe he is a bit of a loner and wanted to stay that way given that he had never married or lived with anyone before..... I suppose we are all different aren't we!!

Every few weeks I would receive the odd email or text - the last one was a text to say he was off on holiday to Ibiza for the week!! OK for some I thought!! He said that he was going away with his mates again before the winter so wasn't really a surprise when he told me he was going. Maybe we can arrange to meet when he gets back I thought...... he did say that he would love to see me when he gets back and he would contact me to make arrangements....... The week Jo was away I received just one text message from him, a photograph of him sunbathing on a sun lounger in front of what looked like a private apartment - nice I thought, but

did wonder who had taken the picture. Its not really a thing I have come across that guys take pictures of guys in a posing position on a sun lounger!! Maybe they do! The text also said that he was back tomorrow and would give me a call......
Good job I didn't hold my breath as I would by now be six foot under in my coffin!!! He never got in touch, so I gave up and chalked it up as another Bad Job!!!

The lesson learnt here for me then is that whatever your colour or creed there are still conmen and time wasters around!!! I didn't want to try a bit of black anyway I said to myself!!! (Even though one of my friends insists that I do...... eventually!!)

Fluff!!!

Another Smoocher!!! (Smooch.com) Mark came across as a man with very few words when I received an email from him saying "Hi there, you're deffo my type!" Mark didn't really have much on his profile apart from saying he was 6'2", separated (did find out that he had been married twice but that's neither here nor there really!) he had 2 kids, non-smoker, worked in engineering (shift work), slim, dark hair (going a little bit two-toned at the sides – well at least he had some hair left!), age 42 and he had the most gorgeous eyes and smile ever!!

We weren't chatting for that long on the website when we agreed to meet half way at a pub we both knew about. Monday evening it was then….. "here we go again" I chuckled to myself as I drove to the rendezvous point. The rain was hammering down and I could hardly see out of the window so had to drive rather slowly to avoid any unnecessary pile-ups!! As I drew nearer to the pub the traffic lights changed to red so I had to stop to let the cars across, how spooky, the lights had changed to let Mark out of the junction – I realised it was him as he had described his silver car to me and there weren't too many of that type about, so HAD to be him!!! My little heart did a bit of a flip when I realised it was him….. oh my!! It was clear that I really did like this guy and yes, he was deffo my type too!!

We both arrived on the car park at the same time, I ran across the car park trying to keep my umbrella up in rather choppy conditions!! Mark also ran for shelter and we said Hi! Went into the pub, bought a drink and sat chatting on some high bar stools placed around a wooden bench like table. He kept telling me that he loved looking deep into my eyes and said he didn't expect to meet anyone quite like me….. I had exceeded his expectations in other words! Great start as far as I was concerned! We had another drink and chatted in total for about 2 hours before going our separate ways….. we both said that we would like to meet again soon. We gave each other a peck on the cheek before we dashing over to our cars. Off we went into the dismal darkness with twinkly eyes and nice thoughts!! (well I did anyway!)

The next day I received a message from Mark saying "Hi, hope you got back home safely, I really liked being with you last night (I am by now expecting a BUT!.... and wasn't wrong!) but think that I am not good enough for you" Well, I wasn't having that was I? I did ask him what he meant and he said that his job wasn't as well paid as mine, he had debts, he hadn't got a car (his ex-wife had their car and he had borrowed one from a friend who was on holiday for a week) he was still paying a mortgage and maintenance for one child. Well, I said to him, these things happen and it's just a timing thing! I told him that I really liked him and would love to see him again. Mark said he would also like to see me again and would travel by train to meet with me next week. So, I was now a happy chappy and looking forward to seeing this gorgeous guy again!!

Each time we met, which was only for a few hours at a time, we both melted as we hugged, kissed and looked into each other's eyes…… wow! He certainly hit THE spot!! – the chemistry was deffo there!!!

On our second date he was showing me some older photographs of himself (ID cards for work) and on one of them he had this little goatee – phew!! He looked very handsome with that and let him know what I thought!! He said in a sort of jokey manner that he would have to grow it back for me...... yikes!! Does this mean he is thinking long term then? (well as long as it takes to grow a goatee at least – that will be a few days then!!) On our third date I picked him up as usual and as I parked my car noticed that he HAD grown this goatee – even more deffo my type!! He was now super gorgeous!! After our third 'get-together' on neutral ground I decided to invite him over for something to eat before he started work – he was on Night shift so didn't start work until 10pm which gave us time to see each other for a few hours. I picked him up from the station one evening, the sun was shining and all he wanted to do was hold my hand and give me lots of pecks on my cheek whilst I was driving..... how romantic, I could really fall for this guy..... BIG time!! I didn't care whether he had a bank balance or not, it didn't matter, he was gorgeous! – we both ended up cooking in the kitchen and if anyone had looked through the window at the time we would have looked like a happily married couple who had been together for a long time..... rather surreal I have to say, but lovely glowing feeling!! Mark even mentioned things like "I will have to fetch my box of tools over to fix that cupboard" he was referring to one of my kitchen cupboards..... nothing cryptic!! As I dropped him off again later that evening to go to work we said that we would arrange a night out and I could stay over at his place (well his parents place which is where he was based until his divorce/separation was sorted!) as they were going to go away soon so the house would be empty.

The date was set and I headed over to his parents place with all my glad rags on.... Heels, lashes, nails, best matching underwear and perfume.... The lot!!! I was really looking forward to seeing him again! A night out on the town, dancing, singing and ...... who knows!! ;-) We had the most fantastic night ever..... we really got on like a house on fire and met some of his friends on our way around the pubs near to where he lived. Mark and I went back to his place with the compulsory kebab (chicken for me and elephant leg for Mark – oh with chips and chilli sauce of course!) The music was on and the scene was set....... Well, all I can say is what an AMAZING night, we really connected and found ourselves on another level of ecstasy which we both commented on....... I don't think we could describe the depth of feeling and intimacy we both had for each other but it was magical!!! I just knew there was something special between us the very first night we met!! "I'm in heaven"

The next morning we got up fairly late, had some breakfast and then went our own ways – Mark had his kids to visit and I had my normal work to do over the weekend. After we had said our goodbyes and kissed each other again I turned to get into my car – Oh my god!!! - what had happened to my car? It had grown a bloody fur coat overnight!!!!!! What on earth..... I stopped in my tracks.... "Ahhh, I know"... I suddenly had a Eureka moment!, "Budgies" that's why I had been hearing budgies from the very early hours of the morning!! I thought it had been the after effects of the Vodka and loud music the night before! It wasn't it was that pet shop a few doors down from the house! The staff who worked there had had the back door open (my car being parked at the back) and rabbit hair – lots of - had blown out of the door and covered the front of my wet car!! I smiled to myself as I realised there is a bit of a theme going

on here…….. RABBITS and RABBIT like behaviour!!!!
……….. I wasn't complaining at all!!

Needless to say this was the last time I actually saw Mark. I had emailed him, text him and called him (answer phone only) but no reply! Here we go again…. I did eventually reply and tell me he was going on holiday to Spain with his parents for a week but nothing else was mentioned! I did say to him that if he didn't want to see me again all he had to do was say so…. I was a big girl and could take it….. I heard nothing at all… the only thing that changed was that his profile was removed from the site we had met on……….. perhaps the "Were Rabbit" off Wallace and Grommit had taken over his bodily functions or maybe he just went back to his wife…… I suppose I will never know!!

ANOTHER LET DOWN!!! ☹

The Weekend Retreat!

I really don't know what it is about the Scottish accent, but it certainly does something to my female senses!! A guy called Robbie had been trying to contact me for weeks on a dating website Click and Flirt it was called!! Every day he sent me a message to see how I was, and asking about my job and would love to meet me as soon as we could. He was from Dundee which was a long way from where I lived, about 5 hours by road I think. He worked on the oil rigs so was "on shore" every 2 weeks, so 2 weeks on the rig and 2 weeks off. Perfect I thought, a good balance between time on my own with friends and family and then two weeks focused on Robbie should this work out long term. The only concern I had really was that he was far away, but distance can be overcome for true love - I could move up to him or he could move south nearer to me which would make things a lot easier!

Robbie was 6'3" tall, red hair (not my normal choice, but hey why not, I've never been out with a red head before! Lol.) Robbie had been married twice before but no kids as a family had just not happened or been planned - that's good I thought he doesn't have any commitments to complicate matters should we end up living together or dare I say it, get married!! Eeek!! Scary thought!! He was a large framed guy which is my preference really as you have something to get hold of on a cold winters night!! ☺ He had a good job so guessed he wouldn't be in any financial difficulties, he had his own house, sexy Scottish accent, attentive, thoughtful and cooked!!! Hey, what more can a girl ask for? Not a lot I don't think!! He had sent me a face picture on my mobile and he looked "OK".

We were chatting for about 3 months before we actually met. He used to ring me most days when he was on the rig and then when he was back on shore I could contact him as there was no signal on the rig! (apparently!) We arranged to meet one weekend when he was back home and duly booked a hotel half way so we could spend some quality time together - he said that if we didn't get on then we could just part ways and if we did then better still! Ok I thought, no pressure! Robbie rang me to say he had booked a hotel in the peak district and sent me the details via text so I could put the postcode into my Satnav... gosh, what did we do before technology? Well we used those things called 'maps'!! Does anyone remember or still use them? We must do as I've not heard of a bunch of Cartographers being made redundant!!

The weekend came and off I drove into the sunset after work to the peak district - the drive had taken Robbie about 3 hours and for me it took about 2.5 hours with the Friday night traffic after work. During our individual car journeys to the hotel we kept in touch by phone tracking each other's progress and getting really excited about seeing each other... at last!!! Robbie had set off earlier on in the day so said he would arrive before me and would have a glass of chilled white wine waiting for me when I got there!! Gosh! A guy who would spoil me and treat me like a lady, an important one in his life..... Is this really happening? Yes it sure was!! I was about 30 minutes away from my destination when I stopped for a bottle of water at a petrol station, I checked my phone to see that I had had a missed call from Robbie and a message on my answer machine. I picked up the message which went something like….. "Hi babes, hope you are OK? I am at the hotel and there has been a slight problem with the hotel booking……" Here we go I thought! Prepare to be driving back home over the next 3 or so hours – yet another blunder!!! The message carried on….. "I must have put the wrong month when I booked the hotel and they don't have any rooms left, the manager has managed to find alternative accommodation which is…….. " and he gave me the directions! Oh ok, I thought, he is genuine and has sorted something out…. I hope! I continued to head for my destination and drove down a narrow country lane to this black and white hotel which was nestled into the mountainside – this looks rather nice I thought. The gardens were really looked after, it was a beautiful sunny day with the odd cloud floating in the sky, white fluffy sheep were grazing in the fields, it was just like being in an episode of postman pat – just missing the black and white cat!!

As I pulled onto the car park looking for a suitable space to park, I caught a glimpse of what I thought was Robbie in my wing mirror. He was exiting the hotel from the bar door to come and greet me!! Mmmm, I think this is him, I muttered to myself…… I continued to straighten my car up and very quickly this huge dark shadow started to stoop down to say hello and give me a peck on my cheek! "Hi" I said, "how are you?" "I am very well thank you darling, especially now I have met you" replied the soft Scottish voice. Yes, it was Robbie, his face looked the same as the photo he had sent to me, but obviously before now I had not actually seen his torso!! He WAS a BIG boy!! I mean, he was tall and wide, both from side to side and front to back!! Oh my, I had NEVER been out with anyone THIS big!!! I smiled, turned my car engine off and extracted myself from my car. Robbie gave me a hug and said that my chilled glass of white wine was waiting for me in the bar….. which it was! We spent a few hours chilling and chatting which was rather pleasant…….. Maybe I should just get to know this guy before making any judgements about his physical appearance (god, how many times have I said that?). He was very tactile and wanted to hold hands and kiss me gently on my neck on a regular basis, which again was rather nice but felt uncomfortable with the locals (who in the main looked like half dead cardboard cut-outs! You know, that sort of grey, dead look people can have in their older years! Bless them! I suppose we will all be there one day! Well not me!! I want to die looking good!! If you know what I mean!) who were taking a keen interest in these newcomers to the village!! Robbie had booked a table in the restaurant for 9 o'clock that evening so an hour before dinner we went up to the room (Robbie went to get my bags from my car and carried them for me) to get freshened up before coming down again. Whilst we were getting ready the TV was on, so no deathly silence moments! and had the odd kiss and cuddle as we passed each other in the narrower parts of the room. Whilst I was in the bathroom putting my makeup on I heard this sort of rumbling sound, "Was that your tum?" I asked Robbie? "No love, but it rhymes with tum". Great, I thought, I wonder how much flatulence his huge colon can hold!!! I bet he could play a good version of "Amazing Grace" unaided by his lung capacity if he chose to!! I chuckled to myself

and told myself to remove that thought out of my head – immediately!!

We went down to dinner as planned and again had a really nice meal followed by more wine afterwards in the main bar, which by midnight had become rather busy and there was a buzz in the air as more guests and locals had emerged from their mountain crevices. Eventually we retired to our room….. I don't really remember that much about the rest of the night, but all I can say is that there was an amount of fumbling that occurred, which in some parts was enjoyable, however can confirm that the relationship was NOT consummated!! Oh my, how the hell could it be with a huge belly the size of a seal pup!? The next morning Robbie asked me if his size bothered me…. I nearly choked on my cup of tea at the time…. How do I answer this one? "Well" I said, "I do have a concern about your health" He responded by explaining that he has a medical check up each year and he is fine as long as he keeps taking his 16 tablets each day for his diabetes! "I didn't know you had diabetes" I said, "It's OK, it's all under control"

That afternoon we went out shopping, had lunch and booked a restaurant for the evening, again very pleasant and chilled, but I was starting to ask myself – could I really fancy this man? Mmmm, not sure! We went back to the hotel to chill, some heavy petting and get ready for the evening. I ran a lovely hot bath full of bubbles and had a lovely soak for half an hour while Robbie lay on the bed (semi clothed) watching TV. As I lay in the bath I could see Robbie in the mirror through a tiny crack in the door. For the 30 minutes I observed him all he did was flick the bloody channels over, rub the bottoms of his legs together and scratch them! He NEVER stopped!! I have to say, the sight of him doing that in his boxers did NOTHING for me! He was starting to annoy me! "Do you have an itch hun?" I asked him, "It's my varicose veins darling" he piped up!! Jeez, is there anything else wrong with this man? Well I suppose the 2 do go hand in hand don't they? This guy seems to be a bit of a health risk to himself and me if we did get together longer term!

We went into the village that evening after I had waited for him to get ready for half an hour (part of which was taken up by burning a pair of trousers he was ironing and setting the smoke detector off! He duly ironed a second pair which did not have a belt to match, and spent the rest of the evening (when he was stood up) pulling his trouser up every 5 minutes! As I reached the bottom of my wine glass in the first pub, it felt as though there had been a piece of paper or something in my wine which I had not seen but felt as I sipped the last drop of wine! "Oops" I said, "There is something in my wine!" I graciously extracted whatever it was from my lips, looked down and to my horror saw it was a FLY!!! I quickly flicked it back into the glass and removed a couple of legs from my lower lip which I had failed to extract earlier!!! Crying out loud!!! How EMBARRASSING!!! I suddenly started to sing to myself "There was an old lady who swallowed a fly, I don't know why she swallowed a fly…. Perhaps she'll die!" Needless to say I was reminded by myself of this incident all night……. I felt quite ill!

We returned to our hotel and room at about midnight that night, I was shattered and still in a state of shock from the fly episode!! Needless to say there was NO fumbling that night and we went to sleep with the TV on! At some point during the early hours I was awoken feeling rather sea sick! It can't be that fly again surely? Nope, it wasn't, it was the bed! The bloody bed was rocking!! I managed to orientate myself in terms of where I was in an unfamiliar surrounding and realised that Robbie was rocking his legs gently up and down about once per second, (sort of like nervous energy) accompanied by his co-ordinated snoring – this was a nightmare!! I lay awake for a couple of hours feeling even more seasick and listening to his awful snoring!! Why the hell do I want to meet someone for a long term relationship and go through this every night? Well, I don't!!! and for that reason I'm OUT!!!!

We parted ways at lunch time on that day and sort of left it that we would arrange to meet up when we could at some point in the future. As I drove home on the Sunday I concluded that this weekend had convinced me that I should stay single!! I am going to give up looking for my soul mate!!! Did I? No..... I decided to still live in HOPE!! ☺

NEXT!!

Do-It-Yourself

Chris was a slim guy, worked in IT and travelled about the country with his job so a busy bunny. He made contact with me first and we chatted for about 6 weeks via t'internet and mobile. He told me he was separated, that's fine I thought I'm in no rush to get married just yet!! He did say on his profile that he was a smoker, however didn't smoke that often and allegedly trying to give it up! He was 5'9" so height was Ok for me, just! ... anything 5'8" and below was not good as I was relatively tall for a woman - 5'9" so I would be able to wear heels that were too high when we went out! Well, if he is the right guy I can live with that - ONLY just! He told me that he wanted to meet with just one girl long term and see what the future brings. He said that he didn't think he would ever get back with his future-ex as they are getting on better now they are separated! Fine with me!

He had brown hair which was peppered with the old grey, he was age 40, but I have to say that he looked lot older than that!! He had 3 sons aged from 15 to 5 - not a problem I thought. Chris had been chomping at the bit to meet with me, but with work commitments and other stuff we had not managed to meet yet! One Saturday he said that he can't wait to meet with me any more and would slip out and meet with me before he went to pick up his 5 year old from his future ex's place. OK I said, and we arranged to meet on B and Q car park - he had suggested this place on a number of occasions which I thought was rather bizarre - maybe he was killing two birds with one stone as he was frequenting the place anyway for his house DIY work!! I arrived about 15 minutes earlier and thought I would have a look in the store to see if there were any bargains!! I like a bargain!! ☺ Anyway, I walked into the store, purchased nothing and swiftly made an exit… Looked at my phone to see if Chris had contacted me "I'm here" said the text, I rang him and explained where I was parked - he said he was just in the store and thought he had seen me - I waited in the car! As he approached I was rather pleased to see that he actually looked like his profile - a little slimmer than I imagined, but that's fine too!! He kept telling me that I was gorgeous and nobody as attractive as me had paid him any attention before!! Mmmm, I thought, I wonder how many heads his future ex-wife had then?

After meeting on a number of occasions over another 4 weeks or so we decided to go for a walk one weekend afternoon when he hadn't got his boys. It was a beautiful autumn day, clear blue skies, no breeze and the leaves on the trees were just turning red and gold. It was a perfect day, as we held hands and walked across the fields towards some woods, which was a well known country walk. As we approached the woods he stopped and kissed me rather raunchily! "Hey up!" I thought, what's this about now? It was very clear to me that his male hormones were rather active at this point and told me he wanted to make love to me in the open air - against a huge oak tree….. Wow!! that's a bit risqué as there were quite a few people about!! Oh well I thought it's a lovely day, and actually my hormones were being aroused so why not, I had been in touch with this guy and seeing him for about 10 weeks now so I think he has been rather patient so far! Off we went into the undergrowth, to find a suitable patch with an oak tree - I just had visions of Robin

Hood and his merry men appearing with their bows and arrows as we cleared away the leaves and twigs.

It was very quiet and you could hear the odd conker fall from the trees and every now and again a cyclist in their lycra would go past on the road which could be seen by us from the bushes!! (too dense to be seen from the road!) After a few awkward moments we managed to get into the swing of things so to speak after sorting out the precautions side of things!! Well, as soon as I had blinked it was all over!!! Great I thought, was that IT? Well, it obviously was as he started to sort himself out and make himself decent again!! Well, how frustrating was that!?!? Oh well, I thought, I'm sure we will have lots of time together in the future… We drove home after having a bite to eat at a country pub, he dropped me off and went on his way to pick up one of his boys from football.

About 10 minutes later I received a text from him…. "Would you totally hate me if I told you I was still married? X" Well, I thought, I know he is still married on paper but has been separated for 18 months, so he told me! I had not been to his pad as his boys were about and it wasn't right to meet them just yet!! Mmmm, I thought does this mean what I think it means? So I text him back… "U mean ur not separated?" Reply…. "Sort of but still married…." What does sort of mean? my text was very short "And?"…. "I wanted to tell you in the car but didn't know how to" Here we go, he must still be living under the same roof!! Another cheat and liar!! I couldn't believe it AGAIN!!! The next text from him read "I'm trying to make thinks work for my kids sake. And will probably go back to her. Feel like I've used you but it wasn't like that. I just wanted some fun with you." So tell me then you guys, why the hell is having fun different from using someone for sex? Answers on a postcard please!! I was fuming at this point so didn't reply to his text….. 5 minutes later I receive another message from him, "You hate me now don't you?" I didn't reply again as I was so mad with him… another text received "Say something please" then another "I won't text you again if you don't want me too" very quickly followed by another "Tell me wot you think of me please" I replied this time "Wot does it matter to u?" "Coz I like you" I received back "And?" I asked. Reply "OK I will leave you alone. Sorry" Well at this point he HAD to have both barrels aimed below the belt!! My final text to him read "Wot the f**k did you want? Just a s**g like most men! U were CRAP anyway! Neva contact me again! ARSEHOLE!" So to this date he hasn't!! If he was wanting to make his marriage work why the hell didn't he put his energies into that instead of lying and cheating with me? I GIVE UP!!! AGAIN!! ☹ Needless to say it was DIY again!!! Good old Ann Summers hey!!! ☺

Hair today...... gone tomorrow!!!

"Wow, he is gorgeous" I said out loud to myself as I opened up an email from this guy who lives in Scotland!! He was 6'1" tall, slim, brown hair with a deep reddish tone which was shoulder length and gorgeous blue eyes!!! He had sent me an email commenting on how gorgeous I looked and he would love to get to know me better. He was looking to date and go with the flow. His name was Roy, single, no children, non-smoker and worked for an electrical company maintaining the supply up in the highlands somewhere!!! Well, if he spends most of his time maintaining pylons, poles and cables he must be rather fit due to his physical work!!! Keep that thought!! ☺

We had been chatting for about 4 months before we actually met, however I had sent him a red and black string before Valentine's day smothered in my favourite perfume and that I would be wearing the rest of the outfit when we meet!!! (a bit saucy I know but he loved it!!)

One particular Friday I was in Edinburgh with work and so we decided to make it a long weekend and I would stay at Roy's until the Sunday evening and fly back home ready for work on the Monday. Sounded like a plan to me!!! I flew to Edinburgh ready for my lunch time meeting, and Roy had said he would pick me up, take me to my meeting, do a bit of shopping before going back to his to start our weekend together!! Fantastic I thought, a guy who could also think as well as being gorgeous!! He had booked the day off work for me so he could do this on the Friday!! Wow! I was impressed!!

The flight was on-time and I rang Roy when I landed to see where I needed to be for him to pick me up easily without getting harassed by parking inspectors and the like!! He told me where to wait and keep a look out for a black VW golf and explained that he was running a little late but shouldn't be too long dependant upon traffic!! Well how many Black VC golfs are there in Edinburgh!!! Bloody loads!!! They must have been a job lot at the dealers recently - they were everywhere!!! Have you ever noticed in life that once somebody makes a comment about a particular vehicle you keep seeing them? E.g White BMW 3 series used to haunt me when I found out my ex-husband had purchased one many years ago!!!

Roy eventually arrived, jumped out of his car to put my case into his boot, gave me a hug and kiss and said wow!! You are just gorgeous! He quickly drove the city centre and dropped me off outside the building where my meeting was and arranged to call him when I had finished in a few hours time!! The meeting seemed to take forever and I found it very hard to concentrate on the business at hand as my mind kept wandering to this Scottish hunk waiting for me!!! AT LAST!! The meeting finished and Roy duly picked my up where he had last dropped me off!! He had stocked up on food and wine ready for our weekend!! Fab!! We drove to his detached 4 bedroom house which was only a few years old however he wanted it to look old and traditional inside as such was in a state of transition!! He certainly was a perfectionist from what I saw!!

Roy explained that his brother was living with him at the moment lives after divorcing from his ex-wife. He wasn't there that weekend as he had been farmed off on a date for the weekend!!!

As soon as we entered the house Roy came towards me and gave me a few kisses and cuddles which was rather nice and reconfirmed that there was a huge spark between us!! After about 10 minutes he said "stop!" and went on to explain that it wasn't for this reason (just sex) that he wanted me there ie suggesting that he wanted something more serious than just a weekend fling!! Fab! Had a few vinos before setting off for what was left of the the afternoon and for the rest of the evening......

We got changed and left the house on foot to the nearest train station and caught the next train into Edinburgh city centre... the journey was a magical 45 minute trip – holding hands, the odd kiss and cuddle sat next to each other and a nice smile when eye contact was made with each other! We were very comfortable and happy in each other's company!

We walked from the station and hit a few pubs (as the Scots do!!) one of the pubs was a real drinkers pub, dark colours with deep oak fittings and old brass beer pumps and about a thousand different types of scotch on the back of the bar!! As we sat chatting and watching the different characters that were about Roy asked if I would ever get married again which rather took me aback!! He quickly went on to say that " that was not a proposal by the way" it was just something he was asking about!! I said I would if the right guy came along. (there endeth that bit of the conversation!)

After a few pubs we went for a lovely meal in a trendy wine bar before catching the last train back to Roy's place.

We called at the off-licence before landing back at Roy's armed with a bottle of wine and bottle of Jack Daniels!!! Jeez, this was going to be a long night!!! We played some music, chilled, carried on drinking and had a few nibbles…… Things did go further than expected and ended up wearing the rest of the valentines outfit for him with stocking and suspenders…. A very raunchy session!!

The next day Roy had planned for us to go and stay in a lovely hotel which had its own night club and restaurant so we didn't have to go far and everything was on hand, spa, pool the lot!! The hotel was about 2 hour's drive away which gave me the opportunity to take in the beautiful Scottish scenery. Even though we had had a huge fry up we stopped off en-route for a home-made ice-cream!!! Scrummy!! So much for the diet hey!!

We eventually arrived at hotel/complex area, booked into the room ready to embark on another steamy session!!! Wow, I can certainly say he knew how to work each of his leg muscles!!! Talk about stamina!!! I was exhausted…. And still had a night of dancing to get through!! We watched a bit of TV (come dine with me) before we decided to get ready and glammed up for the night!!! We took it in turns to get showered and changed - I changed into a posh frock and Roy sort of kept his work boots and jeans on!! Mmmmm OK, no worries…… he is a bit of an 'earthy guy'.

We ventured on down to the restaurant for a lovely meal and wine (beer for Roy) - the entertainment included 2 hen parties (most were half naked! Which sort of distracted Roy from time to time as it would I suppose!) After our meal we went into the bar area for a few drinks - the music as playing and it seemed to be a bit of a 'warm-up' area prior to hitting the 'real' dance floors at the back of the building!! As we remained sitting in the 'warm-up' area a party of about 12 people arrived who seemed to have some sort of disability or seemed to be a sausage roll short of a picnic!!! 'One flew over the cukoos nest' springs to mind!!! And guess what, where did they head for? US!!! For the next half hour we sort of amused them while they amused us on the bit of a dance floor!!!

Oh my, lets get out of here I said!! Roy nodded and we went through to the real clubbing scene!! The music was fantastic and we danced until the early hours of the morning – we crashed out without a raunchy session at about 3am the next morning!! Fab night I thought! Even though the conversation was running a bit dry!!

The next morning we drove back to Roy's place about mid-morning to chill out, however it did feel like it was to 'kill some time' before Roy was due to drive me(to get rid of me more like!) back to the airport to catch my flight – I got a strange feeling that he didn't really want me to be there anymore!!! Roy sat opposite me on the other side of the dining room table for the rest of the day – I did all the approaching to give him a hug and kiss otherwise I just knew he wouldn't have approached me... you get that sinking feeling don't you!! Mmmm, I wonder what's wrong... we talked about the journey to the airport ie flight time and how long it would take to get there and then I touched on the return visit!! Ie invited him to come and stay with me whenever he was free to do so!! Yes, he said he would "give it serious consideration" – legal speak!! That means he's not going to take up my offer of coming over to mine in a few weeks' time!!

He dropped me off at the airport, we gave each other a hug and kiss (quick peck!) and said goodbye – there wasn't much eye contact going on at that time either!!! I rang him after about half an hour to say flight had been delayed, text him to say I really enjoyed being with him… no answer or reply from any of those contacts which was unusual as he always rang or text me back! I just couldn't understand why he had suddenly changed!!!

So he disappeared into the oblivion!! Another one who didn't have the balls to tell you that he didn't want to see you again!! Onwards and upwards yet AGAIN!! A day or so later after taking a shower, to my horror I discovered a rather long leg hair on the back of my leg, just above the stocking line!!! OMG!! It must have been about 6" long!!!! I was HORRIFIED!! Needless to say it was IMMEDIATELY removed with a pair of tweezers and cremated on a mini pyre!! Well suspended over a tea light to be exact!! Could this be the reason why Roy had not wanted to see me again!! We had obviously got intimate when we met so he MUST have seen it!! I was devastated for some time and took me a few weeks to try and get over it!!

About 6 months later I receive a text from Roy asking me how I was…. Very strange!! I could tell it was from him even though I had removed his number from my phone. A few text messages were exchanged which concluded with one from him saying sorry he didn't fancy me!!

Oh well, there is only so much you can say about metal pylons and electricity cables and DIY I suppose……. I need mental stimulation so it probably wouldn't have worked out anyway!!

Money Matters........

I met this guy on the Girls date for Free dating site.... seemed an OK site and got chatting to a few guys as you do when you first join. His name was James, lived about 20 miles away from me, single, had one son aged 12, had his own business, interior design and antiques, and from the way in which he described his life style he was rather minted!!! He had a few horses and hunted on a regular basis - his favourite horse was a 17'2 heavy weight grey gelding who was 8 years old! He had dark hair going grey at the sides "the distinguished look" they describe it as I believe!! He was 6'1" tall, medium build and from his pictures looked ravishing in his white breaches and leather boots!!! Oooer! I hope there is some mutual attraction here!!! He seems like my type of guy!! He had never been married and was just looking to date and see how things went longer term.

On the first date we arranged to meet in a smallish town which was renowned for nice restaurants and wine bars and it wasn't too far away from either of us!! Perfect!! We arranged to meet on a central car park - he would be driving a dark silver range rover so would be easy to spot!! I arrived about 10 minutes early (hate being late), parked my car in a well seen spot and waited!!.... And waited.... And waited.... And waited!!! James had text me to say that he would be a few minutes late.... Eventually he turned up 45 minutes late!! As we walked towards each other he apologised and kissed me on my cheek, put his arm around my waist and directed me to the wine bar we were going to have a snack in!! "OK, I will let him off on this occasion" I said to myself! We had a really pleasant evening and arranged to meet again in the same place and guess what, he was late again!! Only 30 minutes this time!! I quickly realised that this was to be a consistent theme - lack of punctuality!! Oh well, I suppose I could get used to it…. He was rather nice and a good laugh when we did get together!! There was a bit of chemistry there between us, however didn't feel it was going to set the world on fire!! Well, you never know, it may develop! Some people say it does develop over time, but I'm yet to find out exactly what they mean in this respect!! In my opinion, the chemistry is either there from day one or it isn't!!

After a couple months dating James asked me to join him at a friends birthday party - it was in a marquee at his friends small holding. I excitedly accepted the invite and started to plan my attire!! First impressions and all that! I had to look good on his arm!! Especially if I was going to meet his friends and some of his family!! Yikes…. No pressure!! I wore a long strapless black dress with diamante earrings - my hair was worn up also dressed with diamante hair pins which looked rather sexy I have to say!! James picked me up in his range rover, late of course!! And off we drove to the shin-dig!! The marquee was at the end of a long drive way - everything was well organised and a lot of money had been spent to celebrate Carl's 40th birthday bash!!

We all had a great night and spent lots of hours on the dance floor - we eventually rang for a taxi at about 3.00am - another one of James' friends who was on standby to collect people that night. We came back to my place where we had another few drinks before retiring to bed…. At this point the chemistry did start to work (or was it the beer goggles) as we started to kiss and cuddle and get a bit sexual!! We ended up in bed, completely naked making love..... He wasn't very well endowed but it was 'OK' however it didn't have the WOW factor I'm afraid for me!! Anyway we had been in mid-flow for about 20 minutes or so.... When he stopped and said he would be back in a few seconds....!!!! What on earth was he doing now? He returned from the bathroom laden with a large towel which he threw over me and carried on making love!! Oh my!! What a gentleman!! This was to stop the gallons of sweat from dripping all over me..... YUK!! How romantic was that?!!!??? NOT!!!

I'm not sure what time we eventually went to sleep but I can remember wishing he would hurry up!! In fact, I don't think he did 'hurry up' if you get my meaning and gave up!!! Too much alcohol is not always good for the bedroom!!

The next morning I made us a cup of tea and some toast before I drove him back to the farm where the marquee was to pick up his car. We gave each other a peck on the cheek and said our goodbyes with a small hug and went our own separate ways.

After that last encounter with James I decided to throw the towel in (lol - excuse the pun!) and didn't see him again... he just didn't do it for me and I couldn't see anything changing in the near future either!! So, in conclusion, it is the chemistry that matters not the money to me!!!

Let's just give it a couple more tries on the t'internet dating scene, and then if nothing happens I'm going to remove my profile for ever!! (that's assuming it is removed when you do this!! I'm told that on some sites you are still on there to keep the membership numbers up and just says that your profile is being updated if someone tries to contact you!!)

Desperate Dan!!

Dan worked for the Fire Service near to Kings Lynn, aged 48, 5'9", brownish-reddish hair, chunky build with receding hair line. He had no kids and had split from his partner 9 months earlier as she had been found out having an affair with someone affectionately known as the village bike!!!

Our encounter took place on the infamous POF - it was on a day where I was just about to delete my profile when suddenly Dan sent me this lovely email with a couple of pictures telling me how nice I looked. I read his profile which said that he was looking for a serious relationship with one special lady!! He was a Leo (same as ex-husband with the same name!! - is that a good sign or not I wondered?)

Within a period of 7 days or so we had chatted on the phone nearly every day and we seemed to be getting on fine. Conversation flowed and we seemed to have the same sense of humour! Warped!! Dan said that he couldn't wait to meet me and suggested that we got this relationship started as soon as we can with a big bang!!! I.e. an overnight stay in a Premier Inn half way between us - we lived about a 3 hour drive from each other so he thought an hour and a half each between us was a fair deal!! (oh and he told me very early on that he had already had the snip!!) You know, if you met someone in the pub would you very quickly tell them this?!!?? It seems as though once you are on the t'internet it gives you authority to dangle your family jewels in front of who you like and to say what the hell you like!!! Mmmmm,

I thought, well I'm certainly NOT a Premier Inn type of gal!! Before I explained to him that I was happy to meet half way for some lunch he proceeded to ask me if I would book the room!!! WHAT? You are having a laugh aren't you? He explained that he had been left on 2 occasions with a bill for a room and nobody had shown up, hence the reason for asking me to book the room!! Mmmm, does he make a habit of this then?!!!???

I explained that I would be happy to meet half way for lunch, however would not be spending the night with him at a premier inn on the first date!! Eventually he said OK I understand, but 1.5 hours' drive is a long way for a coffee!!! Anyway, we left it that we would meet up in a couple of days once he knew what his 'on-call' work commitments were. That night I received a text saying "Sleep tight sexy lady xxxxxxx thinking about you lots xxxxxxxx" The next morning I text him saying "Hi Dan, how are you today? Thinking ov u xx" the reply came back "Can't wait to see you! Are we going to struggle to drive back home after a coffee? Lol! Why don't we just go for it? Life's too short!! Xxxxxxxx" I declined his offer and said I was a bit old fashioned when it came to first dates!! He told me he would call me after a meeting at 10.00 the next day once he knew what his rota was…. He left me a message at about 3.30pm that day to meet the following day…. Well as I hadn't heard from him I explained that I had now made arrangements to meet with friends and will have to be another time….. I asked him to let me know when he was free next?

Needless to say I never heard from him again….. Obviously this guy was just desperate to get someone into bed and I don't think it really mattered who to be honest!! Oh well! His loss!!!

I've just got 2 words to say to Dan!!!! FOR COFFEE!!!

To Loo's Le Truck!!

David from Cardiff!! Well what can I say!! He was gorgeous, blonde curly hair, shoulder length, blue eyes, cheeky smile, clean shaven (face I mean!!) a very sexy welsh accent, 5'11" tall, slim to medium build, non-smoker and was a trucker!!!

We had started to chat on Badoo and exchanged mobile numbers fairly early on and would chat not and again about life in general and what he was up to! Very chilled and no pressure to meet him. Every now and again he would text me to say he was in my neck of the woods and would be staying over at a lorry park not far from me, and if I was free would I like to join him!!! (and not for pie, chips and gravy either!!) I said it would be good to meet him at some point but a night in his cab didn't really appeal at this stage.

He laughed at me and said don't be a spoil sport and that I knew I wanted him!!! I laughed and said don't be cheeky!! Anyway to cut a long story short, we eventually met in a pub near to me as he was overnight again with work. We purchased a drink from the bar and found somewhere cosy to sit and chat and get to know each other better! We were chatting for about an hour in total and it must have been every 5 minutes that he asked me to meet with him in the disabled toilet for sex!! I kept shrugging it off and shyly laughing at him!!! Eventually, as he started to get on my nerves, I said "OK then, you go in first and I will be with you in a few minutes so it didn't look quite as obvious!"

OK he said, he was like a dog with 2 bones!! So excited!!
He gave me a peck on my cheek before he made his way
through the pub towards the disabled toilets. He opened the
door and turned around to give me a cheeky wink before he
entered the room and closed the door behind him!!!

I left it a few minutes before I stood up and walked towards
the disabled toilet…. And carried on walking to the exit
door!!! Well, if he thinks that I'm about to join the "Handy
Rail Club" i.e. instead of the "Mile High Club" or "125
Club" he's got another think coming!! I jumped into my car
and drove home which was only about 5 minutes away!!

I text him "Keep on trucking baby"…… I obviously didn't
hear from him ever again!! Lmao!! (Laughing My Ass Off)
I wonder how long he stayed in there before he cottoned on
to the fact that I wasn't going to make an appearance!! Doh!!
Life is full of surprises is it not? ☺

Conclusion

In terms of relationships, what is right and what is real has left me in a stage of confusion! When I take time to think about the notion of marriage and one partner for life 'it' just doesn't stack up based on the encounters that are happening, I'm sure around the world!

Are all men either boring, plonkers, liars or cheats? Is it that when we do find THE one who is exciting, dynamic, fun, sexy and passionate that cheating is also part of the package? I wait to be proven wrong! ☺

So, where do I go from here?

To be honest, I have no idea! Just that I continue to hope (NB not look, 'cos that doesn't work!) that those in control of the Universe and the powers that be, do eventually direct my new soul mate towards me and our paths cross or emails exchange! Let's wait and see what the next chapter of my life brings!..............

Who knows, it CAN ONLY GET BETTER! ☺............
Can't it??? ☹